the GEO Principle

God in Every Occupation
means purpose for every job
– *even yours!*

TOM BENGTSON

The GEO Principle: God in Every Occupation
means purpose for every job – *even yours!*

www.GEOprinciple.com

Inspiration/business/self-help

First edition
January 2009

Published by:
NFR Communications, Inc.
7400 Metro Blvd., No. 217
Minneapolis, MN 55439

Library of Congress Control Number: 2008940455

ISBN: 978-0-975-4134-3-2

Cover and book design by:
Traditions Communications LLC
www.TraditionsCommunications.com

Printed in the United States of America.

TABLE OF CONTENTS

the GEO Principle

God in Every Occupation
means purpose for every job
– even yours!

TOM BENGTSON

CHAPTER ONE

Bring God to Work

LOTS OF PEOPLE bring their lunch to work, or a briefcase, or a laptop computer, but how many people think about bringing God to work? Anyone could, although it seems few people do.

Most working Americans spend half their waking lives – or more – on the job. That's a lot of time to be keeping God at bay. If God is important in your life, then he should be alive in the place where you spend a good portion of your time, on the job. Yet it is common to think of God as a sick child or a pet, something that is best kept at home.

Many people who share fellowship and a sign of peace at Sunday worship go to work Monday morning determined to get ahead no matter what that means for the people around them. Others work all day promoting the products of a hedonistic culture, making sure to quit by 5:30 so they can get home in time for evening services or choir practice.

While it's common today to divide life into distinct periods of faith-filled living and secular living, it wasn't always like that. A century or more ago, when a significant portion of the population lived in rural areas or in small towns, far fewer people had a choice about when and where to live their faith. If you live where you work, as did nineteenth century farmers and shopkeepers, there isn't much decision to make about living your faith at work. If you have any faith at all you are going to live it at work because the distinction between home life and work life is inconsequential. When your farm is your home, if you are living your faith at home, you are living it at work.

Today the decision about where to live your faith is much more pronounced. Like a wedge, industrial, commercial and technical progress over the last century has put distance between home and workplace; participants in today's workforce confront a real decision about where to live their faith. If you had asked a nineteenth century farmer whether he brings his faith to work, he would have given you a puzzled look; the question simply would not have made any sense. Today, however, such a question is very real. Are you bringing God to work? If not, why not?

Nearly everyone works in America. Stay-at-home moms work 24/7; students know that learning is serious work, and many senior citizens pour tremendous effort into volunteer work. But the question about whether to bring God to work resonates particularly with people who have a paying job, people who go somewhere to work, people pursuing careers and corporate success. Every day, on their way to work, employees make a decision – consciously or subconsciously – about whether to bring God with them.

Faith, of course, is a great gift; if you are living your faith at home, you know what it can do for you. Knowing God is the way to know purpose in life. Faith brings inner peace; it guides your interaction with others; it gives you the moral compass to make difficult decisions, and it gives you the fortitude to persevere through difficult situations. All of these benefits can be useful in the workplace.

If you were to go camping in the woods, and you had a really good compass, you wouldn't leave it at home. You'd take it with you. If you work and you have faith, you are like that camper. Just as it seems obvious he should bring the compass with him into the woods, it is clear that you should take your faith with you into the workplace.

The GEO Principle is about bringing God to work. It is a pro-active principle about filling the workplace with the faith-filled light of home. Where there is no light there is darkness, and too many businesses are operating in the dark because faith-filled employees leave their faith at home. Mark (4:21) quotes Jesus asking: "Is a lamp brought in to be placed under a bushel basket?" Of course not! A light is to be placed where everyone can see it. As an essential tool of harvest some 2,000 years ago, the GEO Principle sees the basket as a symbol for commerce. Too many people who have the light within them cover that light up when they enter the world of commerce. While they live devoted lives at home, they live like agnostics at work. God invites us to let that light shine all day long, at home and at work.

Think about what happens to a burning flame under a bushel basket. Either the flame goes out or it burns away the basket and no longer remains hidden. The light within us is like that. Eventually, either darkness or light takes over. If you suppress the light at work long enough, the flame may go out, in which case it wouldn't even be available to illuminate your way at home. The GEO Principle is about burning away that bushel basket at work so your professional colleagues benefit from the light, as well as your family and neighbors at home. Perhaps the light is flickering or beginning to smolder within. You can revive the flame by making a commitment to bring God to work.

The GEO Principle is about bringing God into every moment of the day, like that nineteenth century farmer who made no distinction between home life and work life. And if you work, there is only one way God is going to get into every moment: You have to bring him to the job. Whether you practice your occupation in an office, a factory or a store, you can bring God to work.

God makes it very easy for us because he's already there. God is everywhere, so he is already at your office. His omnipresence, however, doesn't get you off the hook. The GEO Principle focuses on the fact that God works with people like you to accomplish his will. Scripture gives us incredible examples of God working with ordinary people in order to make himself known to the world. God, for example, could have preserved the human race any number of ways on his own, but he chose to work with Noah. God could have freed the Israelites from Egypt by himself, but he chose to work with Moses. And God could have sent his son into our world without any help, but he chose to work with Mary. God chose to work with each of these people, even Moses who initially wasn't willing. Furthermore, each of these people could have rejected God outright, but they worked with him even though they didn't understand what the results would be.

The GEO Principle is based on the premise that God is calling you to work with him to make him known throughout the world, including your place of work. If you know you have faith, then consider yourself chosen. John 15:16 makes it clear: "You did not choose me, but I chose you and appointed you that you should go and bear fruit…"

Just think what our world might be like if everyone brought God to work. Honesty and openness would lead to greater levels of trust between colleagues. Greater levels of trust mean less required supervision, which could lead to fewer layers of management and, ultimately, greater levels of work satisfaction, lower costs, better prices for customers and higher returns for shareholders. Workers who respect the dignity of their colleagues don't discriminate or harass. Employees who take pride in their work produce better products and provide better service. This could result in safer goods and happier customers. Auditors and regulators would have little to do. The business section of our nation's newspapers would be filled with success stories rather than chronicles of corporate scandal. Living your faith at work, clearly, is not only good for you, but it also is good for your company and the world.

The GEO Principle will help you to bring God to work. Don't leave him at home any more. This book will give you ideas about what to do. Read through the entire book and spend time with the questions at the end of each chapter. Then, form or join a study group so you can read it with others and benefit from their insight. Talk about each GEO Principle concept in the context of your own experience and situation. Supplement your discussion by working through the material suggested for further consideration. You will find interaction between study group members will aid your discernment. Thought and discussion are vital steps for turning the GEO Principle into reality.

Consider 〉 〉 〉

1. What do you think it was like to work in the United States in the late 1800s or earlier? Was it easier then for people to live their faith in the workplace than it is today?

2. What barriers keep you from bringing God to work?

3. How would today's workplace change if everyone brought God to their occupation?

ACTION STEP 〉 〉 〉

Commit yourself to doing something that reduces the distinction between home life and work life. For example, share your work with your family; consider teaching your children some component of your profession or trade. At a minimum, make sure your workstation includes a photo of your family.

For Further Consideration, Read 〉 〉 〉

Mark, Chapter 4

CHAPTER TWO

What's the Purpose of Work?

WHY DO WE go to work, anyway? Most people think work is about making money, but the GEO Principle proposes something different. Let's consider why we work in the first place. Before considering what it means to bring God to work, it's important to understand the purpose of work.

Matthew gives us a starting point with his story about a wealthy man who gives three servants some money before going on a journey (25:14-30). He gives one of them five coins. He gives another servant two coins and a third servant is given one coin. When the man returns, he rewards the first two servants for doubling his money while he was away; he punishes the third servant who did nothing with his coin.

The story reveals, first, that we are supposed to work. The master clearly expects all three of the men to work. This is a relatively easy message to accept; most of us don't challenge the notion today that we are supposed to work, even if we'd rather not. Second, the story reveals that providing for self is not the purpose of work. The master provided for each of the workers; they did not need to provide for themselves. Other gospel accounts (Matthew 6:31-33 and

Luke 12:28-31) reinforce the idea. They tell us that if we seek God first, he will provide. Just as the master gave each of those servants what they needed, scripture repeatedly assures that God will give us what we need. The only miracle other than the Resurrection described in all four gospels is the one about Jesus feeding thousands of people with five loaves of bread and two fish. Consider further that before the fall to sin in Genesis, God clearly provided. Adam and Eve had everything they needed, yet they still had work; they designated names and ruled over the animals. The message is clear: God provides but he still expects people to work.

This raises the question: If the purpose of work isn't to provide, then what is it?

This question is vexing because almost everyone ties work to compensation, which is used to provide for self and family. Many people would say they are only working for the money. If not for the pay, then work has no meaning. But upon further consideration, the link between compensation and work deteriorates.

Many people perform extremely valuable work, for example, and don't get paid a dime. Think about the stay-at-home parent or the nursing home volunteer or the active member of the PTA. These folks do important work and never collect a paycheck. Furthermore, there are many people who continue to collect compensation long after their work is done. An author may stop writing on the book's last page but collect royalties for years to come. Movie stars may collect payments from films they made decades ago.

And the nine-to-five set understands; they know that the relationship between work and compensation is not uniformly equitable. Teachers make small salaries but perform important work. Athletes and actors perform non-essential work and can earn a king's ransom. And while hard work remains one of the key ingredients to getting ahead, it does not guarantee success. Talk to any salesman who has been in business through a couple of economic cycles. If the economy is slow, the hardest working salesperson will have difficulty matching numbers posted in better times when he didn't have to work as hard.

So while most people get jobs to make money, the relationship between work and money is murky. The true purpose of work is actually much clearer.

The purpose of work is to grow closer to God.

In Matthew's gospel, those two servants who worked entered into a deeper relationship with their master. They were invited to "enter into the joy of your lord." The servant who did not work, on the other hand, found himself cut off from his master. That servant did not get to enjoy an ongoing relationship with his master; he was thrown into "the outer darkness." This story is a powerful validation of work; through work, we enter into deeper, ongoing relationship with our Master.

The GEO Principle contends this is true even for people who deny the existence of God. All people define and refine their relationship with God at work whether they believe in him or not. Belief does not determine whether something is true. Consider that Pilate was unclear about truth (John 18:38) but still enjoyed considerable authority, which came from God. He understood his authority even if he didn't understand its source. God provides for everyone, even the people who are unclear about where the provisions come from.

The relationship between God and working people can be understood by considering the relationship between a parent and child.

Consider the father who asks his seven-year-old son to help him clean the garage. Any adult would be able to clean out a garage much more efficiently without a little kid afoot, yet a father is inclined to ask his child to help. Why? Because the father wants the child to grow closer to him; the father wants a deeper relationship with his son. Work, however unevenly distributed, gives the father what he really wants and the child what he really needs – not a cleaner garage but a closer relationship.

Consider a second example. A mother is making a cake. Her five-year-old daughter is playing in the next room. Mom invites her to join her in the kitchen. "Will you help me bake a cake?" The child jumps with excitement and the two of them spend a pleasant hour together reading a recipe, measuring and mixing ingredients, baking and preparing a delectable frosting. Do you think this woman really needed help making a cake? Of course she didn't. She asked the child to join her in order to further develop the relationship between them. At the end of the day, the child can say she helped to bake a cake but what she really did was grow closer to her mom.

These two stories are analogies for the relationship between God and people in the workforce. God asks us to work not because he needs help providing for us, but because he wants us to get to know him better. He doesn't need our help, but he wants our help because the work offers an opportunity for us to grow closer to him.

And, although we can claim that we "earn" our rent and food because we actually do work, it is really God who provides for our home and meals. We would be foolish to ignore God's hand in our work, just as the boy would be foolish to claim he cleaned the garage on his own, or the girl would be silly to say she baked the cake by herself.

Part of the reason any parent wants to spend time with a child is because a parent wants to help the child to grow up. We parents want to help them become like us, that is, adults. We want to help them become who they are supposed to be. That's the same reason God wants us to spend time with him, so that we become who we are supposed to be, so that we become a little more like him. God, after all, was the first worker; he created the universe. By working, we imitate him. If you are a father or a mother, think of how you felt when you saw your son or daughter do something on their own for the first time. Think of how you felt when your daughter measured the baking ingredients by herself, on her own, for the first time; or think of how you felt the first time your boy sorted out the nuts from the bolts by himself, on his own. You felt great! You were happy – not because of the cake or the hardware, but because by working successfully the child showed he or she was maturing, becoming a little more like you, advancing toward the person they were meant to be.

If you've worked with someone for a long period of time, you know what it can do for a relationship. Friendships are commonly formed on the job because people build unique bonds when they work together. People can really get to know each other when they work on a project together, particularly if they are creating something – even more so if they have been at if for a long time, weathering bad times and challenges together, as well as victories and celebrations. If you bring God to work, you obtain the opportunity to get to know him in a way you never would have had you left him on the kitchen table like a forgotten lunch pail.

Now that we have laid a foundation for the purpose of work, let's look at what it means to bring God to work.

Consider ❭ ❭ ❭

1. Have you ever helped a child learn to do something? How did it make you feel?

2. Have you worked with anyone for a long time? How does your relationship with that person affect your work?

3. How would your attitude about your job change if you believed the primary purpose of work is to grow closer to God?

ACTION STEP ❭ ❭ ❭

Write down all the ways God provides for you and your family.

For Further Consideration, Read ❭ ❭ ❭

Matthew, Chapter 25

CHAPTER THREE

Offer Up Your Best

GOD WAS THE first worker and we can read about his first recorded job in the initial chapters of Genesis. He set an example of working hard as he created the universe. It was quality work; the Garden of Eden was a nice place, by all accounts.

When we work, we are imitating God. It's a noble endeavor that makes us a little bit like the Creator. We build our relationship with God as we imitate him. Think about what it means to do something for the sake of a relationship, rather than solely for the money. A shoe-maker, for example, might make good shoes all day long but, when it comes to making a pair of shoes for the love of his life on her birthday, you can bet he will work a little harder on that particular pair. He will do his best work for her because of the relationship. When we work for the sake of our relationship with God, we naturally work a little more diligently.

God wants our best work. We know from Genesis 4 that God makes distinctions between good offerings and mediocre ones. God praised the offering from Abel's work, but was unsatisfied with Cain's offering.

The world wants your best work, too. In today's highly competitive, global marketplace, only the best work survives. Companies that do mediocre work typically don't last very long. That means that every employee needs to be doing his or her best work.

A foundational premise of your effort should be the success of your enterprise. It is very important that you and your company succeed. Any business venture, even a very small one, has people depending upon it. There are customers who want to buy your products, there are vendors whose livelihood depends upon your business, there are employees who need to make a living, and there are shareholders who are looking for return on their investments. All of these people are better off if your company is reliably fruitful, a prospect dependent upon your best work.

The non-profit sector does a world of good, but there could not be a non-profit sector without a robust for-profit sector. Companies like the one you work for have to make money, pay employees and vendors, and return profit to shareholders before anyone can donate charitably to a non-profit organization.

And don't forget that a successful commercial sector is also essential for the maintenance of our roads, national defense and welfare safety net. If your company or store doesn't make money, there won't be any taxes to fund these shared responsibilities. If your employer doesn't make money, that's one less enterprise contributing taxes to fund local, state and federal programs.

Companies comprised of employees who consistently underperform don't survive. Competitors take over their market, sometimes to the point that the inferior company goes out of business. Work is a serious endeavor; the consequences of shoddy or incomplete work are significant. Perhaps those consequences were more obvious on the farm, where late planting or poor weed control result in diminished harvest. Depending on where you work, the consequences of mediocre work today may be masked to some degree, but they are real.

And it doesn't do any good to complain about a competitor. Competition is okay. In fact, consumers benefit from competition.

Employees do to, because competition keeps those of us in the workforce sharp. Competition provides a measure so that work can be impartially judged as either good or insufficient.

Faith-filled members of the workforce can be – and should be – competitive. It is a mistake to believe that faith-filled people are timid or mild. God-fearing people are not pushovers – or if they are, it has nothing to do with their faith. Vigorous competition is part and parcel of the commercial arena. Organizational excellence doesn't happen in a vacuum; competition forces organizations to figure out how to improve.

Employees intent on bringing God to work don't have to wonder whether they should compete, they just need to focus on competing fairly. Competitors should be respected, not disparaged. Marketing messages should focus on the benefits of your solution, not the deficiencies of the competitor's product. Honesty should be a fundamental principle of your company's communication.

It is easy to understand how a manager sets the tone for his or her department. People look to their supervisors for direction about what's acceptable and what's not. Regardless of the title you hold, however, understand that everyone manages something. Entry-level employees have to manage the particular responsibilities of their job, even if they don't get a lot of recognition or compensation for it. But responsibilities are serious nonetheless, regardless of whether you are the night watchman or the CEO.

And no matter what position you hold in the company, you can benefit from the counsel Jesus gives Peter at Luke 22:32. He says: "I have prayed that your own faith may not fail; and once you have turned back, you must strengthen your brothers." From this advice, we can learn something about what Jesus expects from a manager.

Jesus gives Peter a management role and then defines that role in a context of service. Jesus instructs Peter to "strengthen your brothers." Peter's job is to help the other apostles succeed. Jesus doesn't say, "Go back and let the others serve you."

If you have employees reporting to you, you might be tempted to think that management is about ordering others around, living the high life on an ample expense account, maybe even flying around on a corporate jet. Directing others, spending money and traveling efficiently are important, but Jesus doesn't mention those things. In addition to his advice to Peter in Luke's Gospel, consider his instruction in Matthew 20:26. He says: "…whoever desires to become great among you, let him be your servant."

While it may be common in the corporate world to define management ranks in terms of perquisites, compensation and staff size, Jesus talks about it in terms of serving others. This is incredibly good news for those who are looking to move up in their career. You don't have to wait to be promoted to be a manager. You are a manager right now by virtue of the fact that you serve others.

Consider ❱ ❱ ❱

1. Everyone manages something at work; what do you manage?

2. Are you doing your best work, day in and day out? If not, what would it take to improve?

3. How does your relationship with God affect the quality of your work?

4. How competitive is your work environment? What attitude do you have about your competitors?

ACTION STEPS ❱ ❱ ❱

1. Review your job description, or if you don't have one, write one for yourself. Consider how you are performing in each aspect of your job and come up with ways to improve.

2. Implement at least three concrete things you can do to be a servant to your work colleagues.

3. Ask your manager what he or she thinks it takes to be an effective manager and assess whether you can apply any portions of the answer to your own work. (Do you have a close enough relationship with your manager to ask such a question? If not, work on building a closer relationship with your manager.)

For Further Consideration, Read ❱ ❱ ❱

The Book of Genesis, Chapters 1 – 11

CHAPTER FOUR

Pay Attention to Your Boss

IN ADDITION TO being managers, some people are leaders. Successful companies need successful leadership, which may
come from you or from others. Since most of us are followers,
the example of a leader in any organization is particularly important. Employees watch their managers and bosses because of the
profound ability they have to affect their lives and the lives of those
around them. In the best environments, those managers and bosses
are true leaders.

Best-selling author and business consultant Patrick Lencioni
says a business leader is like a minister:

*All managers can, and really should, view their work as a min-
istry. A service to others. By helping people find fulfillment in their
work, and helping them succeed in whatever they're doing, a manager
can have a profound impact on the emotional, financial, physical and
spiritual health of workers and their families. They can also create an
environment where employees do the same for their peers, giving them
a sort of ministry of their own. All of which is nothing short of a gift
from God.*[1]

Because of the significant impact business leaders can have on so many people, it is particularly important that they bring God to work. Entry-level and middle-management level participants in the commercial world should have the example of their leaders bringing God to work before they can be realistically expected to do so themselves.

David Gergen, director of the Center for Public Leadership at Harvard University, called a manager's example one of the most important components of effective leadership. "You send out signals," he said. "Other people take their cues from that person. If the leader is dishonest, cuts corners, is shady, lacks character and runs the company that way, others are going to take their cues from that and they will engage in a lot of shady practices. By contrast, if the leader is a model of rectitude and integrity, and also draws strength from his religious views – that is what will encourage others to think there is something there that I would like to emulate."[2] Gergen, an editor-at-large for *U.S. News & World Report*, should know, having worked for presidents Nixon, Ford, Reagan and Clinton.

No matter what job you hold at your company, you should pay attention to your boss. Jesus' statement in Luke (6:40) that "no disciple is superior to the teacher…" is an affirmation of hierarchy and validates the notion that we should pay attention to our superiors. Some roles, by their nature, give people authority over others. Even as companies are generally flattening or reducing management layers, hierarchal structure remains important. Someone has to be the boss.

As an entry-level employee or the person with the least seniority, it can be difficult to muster the respect due a manager. It is human nature to begrudge a boss, at least to some extent. Sometimes, bosses bring this upon themselves. Researchers at Florida State University surveyed more than seven hundred people in business: 39 percent of them said their boss doesn't keep promises; 24 percent said the boss invades their privacy and 23 percent said their boss blames others to cover up their own mistakes.[3] Certainly there are a lot of bad bosses out there. Nonetheless, you need to respect yours. If you find it impossible to respect your boss, a job change might be in order.

Think of Matthew 23:2-3 where Jesus instructs his disciples to respect the scribes and Pharisees because of the authority they hold, not because of their example. The scribes and Pharisees were like bad bosses. Jesus didn't tell his disciples to ignore them; he asked them to honor the authority due them, given their role. But he also did not ignore the fact that they were foolhardy; that's why he warned against imitating them. If your boss asks you to do something legitimate, you need to do it. But if he is a fool, you don't need to act like one yourself.

Because God gives every person profound human dignity, the way to show love for others is to respect that dignity. Whether you are at the top of the organization or the bottom, your best work must be marked by respect for the dignity of those around you. The Golden Rule gives you valuable direction: Treat others as you would like to be treated. Specifically, consider these guidelines:

First, treat those around you as partners. Never look down on anyone. Seniority and rank are very real in many organizations, so for most people this means amplifying the meaning of that rank for those who hold posts above you, and ignoring it for people who hold the same rank or lower rank as you do. Respect the meaning of titles, but don't lord your title over anyone. If you have direct reports, you need to take the responsibility inherent in your own title very seriously, but look at those employees as partners more than subordinates.

Second, help those around you succeed. If you succeeded at something, share the key to that success with others. Information and knowledge that you find useful should be shared with others in the organization who might also benefit from them. If you have employees, make sure they get the training they need. Don't make them struggle with antiquated equipment or unrealistic goals. Pair employees up with associates and vendors who can help them become winners.

Third, compensate fairly. Good managers wish to share the company's prosperity with employees; poor managers view employees as a necessary expense to be negotiated to the lowest rate possible. An employer should seriously consider the appropriate compensation level for every job. Employers should not assume they are offering a just wage based merely on the agreement of the employee. People who lack education or negotiating skills may unwittingly accept a lower wage than others doing comparable work. Determining an appropriate compensation level for any job should include consideration of such factors as market conditions, the company's own levels of profit, and the employee's experience and skill level.

Fourth, keep your promises. Commitments made to colleagues and customers need to be fulfilled. Reputations suffer at the hand of regularly broken promises. Trust is not easily restored. Colleagues who don't trust you on work affairs will never trust you on bigger things, like eternity or the meaning of life. People won't give you an opportunity to share your faith if you abuse the work opportunities you get first.

Fifth, be honest. Consider whether your corporate culture promotes honesty. How forthcoming are you with vendors and employees? Are the company's financials transparent? Do you clearly explain pricing for your service or product? Is your company's marketing and advertising honest? One of the reasons it is important to be honest with customers is because if colleagues know you'll lie to a customer, they know you'll probably lie to them.

Recall that God himself is our model in the workplace. Do you think that Jesus, when making furniture in his carpentry shop, ignored those around him, lied to customers and made promises he had no intention of keeping? Of course he didn't, and neither should we.

While these kinds of best practices generally result in more profitable business, they do not guarantee success. Homebanc Corporation of Atlanta was a large financial services company that touted itself as a Christian organization; it filed for bankruptcy in August 2007. The credit crunch and the impact of the subprime mortgage fiasco hit the company like any other. For Homebanc, it was too much and 1,100 people lost their jobs.

Gergen commented about this, too. "Religious faith is not a guarantee of good leadership," he said. "You can't say that someone who is spiritually rooted will be a good leader, although you often find that good leaders are spiritually rooted."

A faith commitment is not a hedge against inflation or a protection against recession. Matthew 5:45 notes "...he makes his sun rise on the evil and the good, and sends rain on the just and the unjust." Welcoming God into your workplace is no different from welcoming God into your home. Families made up of faith-filled people suffer as much as families made up of people who are ambivalent about their faith. The point of living your faith at home and at work is not to avoid suffering, but to enter into deeper relationship with God.

Remember, God provides. If you have viewed work for years as a means of providing for yourself, you may find it difficult to acknowledge God as the real provider. While it might be easy to *say* "God provides," it is something else to really *believe* it. The more you allow yourself to love those around you at work, however, the easier it will become to acknowledge God as provider. Love your colleagues because God loves you; work to grow closer to God.

Consider ❱ ❱ ❱

1. Is your boss a leader? Why or why not? Are you a leader?

2. Do you respect the dignity of those with whom you work?

3. How are you helping your colleagues to succeed?

ACTION STEPS ❱ ❱ ❱

1. Identify at least two colleagues who could benefit from your help; take steps to help them advance in their careers.

2. Discuss with colleagues how your products are marketed. If your company relies on deception, disparagement, sexism or negative cultural stereotypes to market its products, challenge those responsible to come up with something different.

For Further Consideration, Read ❱ ❱ ❱

The Three Signs of a Miserable Job: A Fable for Managers (and Their Employees) by Patrick Lencioni (Jossey-Bass, 2007)

CHAPTER FIVE

Your Office is Ready for God

YOU CAN BRING God to your workplace even if it seems secular and interested only in profit. Remember, Jesus was born in a stable, surrounded by farm animals. He spent his first days sleeping on a bed of straw. While that stable was not a holy place before he arrived, it was not an immoral place. Neither the shepherds nor animals at the stable expected him, yet they were hospitable toward him. Just as Mary and Joseph brought Christ to the stable, you can bring God to any environment that is not overtly hostile to him.

The nativity story is reassuring. God did fine in a lowly stable; he will do fine in your shop. God is comfortable in almost any setting – a place does not need to be holy, nor does it need to be filled with people who are expecting God, nor people who know they are looking for God. This describes the vast majority of workplaces.

In fact, early twenty-first century Western culture offers a work environment that may be more eager to consider God than ever. Several events and cultural factors come together these days, creating an environment that is receptive to workplace evangelization. Consider:

❯ The terrorist attacks on September 11, 2001 brought home

the message that life is precious. Those people in the World Trade Center were doing their jobs and it all came to an end, suddenly and without warning. The event forces us to confront our own mortality, which inevitably raises questions about God and belief. Furthermore, the event linked those questions to the workplace.

❱ Many people in the workplace are outraged by the corporate scandals that seem to dominate the headlines. One of the ways people rebel against the greed exemplified by the scandals surrounding the bailout of Fannie Mae, Freddie Mac and Wall Street investment firms is by considering morality as it applies to the work environment.

❱ The push for diversity, which is so popular in corporate America, actually makes it easier to overtly live your faith. In the past, social pressures homogenized. Everyone was expected to be the same and people were asked to keep quiet about differences. Now, we celebrate differences. A workplace that tolerates all lifestyles and ideas cannot logically suppress peoples' ideas about God.

❱ Many companies offer an employee assistance program, which is a kind of counseling service to which employees can turn for advice and comfort. The service gives employees an option for seeking counseling on virtually any topic, including questions about mortality, eternity and life fulfillment. The counselor is likely to steer an employee to a pastor or clergyman if appropriate, but the service opens up the possibility of people bringing their deep philosophical questions to work.

❱ Many people already are practicing very demanding religions in their workplaces. Taxi-drivers who refuse to transport customers carrying alcohol, employees demanding specified times for prayer during the work day, pharmacists who refuse to sell particular products, and check-out clerks who refuse to handle certain grocery items have all made the news. In many cases, the employers go to extraordinary lengths to accommodate the employee. If a workplace can accept these kinds of practices, it should be easy for employees to bring God to work in a far less disruptive manner.

❱ Politicians, who go a long way toward setting cultural norms, now talk openly about their faith. President Carter frankly professed his Baptist beliefs. President Reagan was candid about his faith. And President George W. Bush is comfortable referring to his relationship with God. Presidential candidates readily invoke their faith in God during debates, speeches and interviews.

The fact of the matter is, you have more opportunity to shape the environment at your workplace than most workers in the past ever had. In the mid-twentieth century, when the number of competent workers far out-numbered the supply of good jobs, workers were afraid to say anything that might make waves. But today, competent workers are in short supply. If you are one of them, you can speak your mind, of course while honoring the dictates of respectability and good nature. Our culture is inviting you to be yourself. If you want to bring God to work, you have tremendous freedom to do so.

So what's it like to actually work as if God were at your side? How does a person bring God to work? Chapter six begins to dig into these questions.

Consider ❱ ❱ ❱

1. Is anyone at your workplace trying to practice their faith in an overt way? What are they doing? Do they make you uncomfortable?

2. Have events such as 9-11 or the meltdown of the financial markets affected your thinking about the workplace and your role in it?

3. What does "diversity" mean to you? Is diversity helpful in the workplace? Does it apply to people with different ideas about God?

ACTION STEP ❱ ❱ ❱

Add something to your desk, cubicle, office or workstation that communicates your faith commitment. This might be an icon, holy card, Bible, cross or even a family picture taken at a religious event.

For Further Consideration, Read ❱ ❱ ❱

The Acts of the Apostles

CHAPTER SIX

First Step to Bringing God to Work: Prayer

BRINGING GOD TO work means introducing him to those around you. A successful introduction is dependent upon a trusting relationship between parties. You have to build relationships with those around you before you can expect to introduce them to God. Build those relationships by working in a manner that dignifies your colleagues, as counseled in chapters three and four.

Consider, however, that even before you can introduce God to someone else, you have to know him yourself. You build a relationship with God the same way you build a relationship with anyone – through communication. Just as you would confide in a friend, confide in God. Just as you would talk to a neighbor, talk to God. This communication is called prayer.

Prayer can take many forms but consider these four ideas for workplace prayer.

First, start every day – weekday or weekend – with a little prayer of gratitude. This prayer can take place while you are still lying in bed, perhaps moments after you have clicked off the alarm. Or you could build prayers of gratitude into established morning rituals that may involve prayer on your knees or meditative reading in a comfortable chair. Regardless of the format, take time first thing every day to thank God for blessings in your life, including your work. Thank God for providing for you and your family.

Second, take a few minutes to pray during your work commute. If you are driving to work, turn off the radio, at least for a few minutes. Roll up the windows and create a sanctuary in your car. If you are taking a bus or a train to work, put your newspaper down and close your eyes. Ignore all the advertisements that surround you; try to shut out all the messages that scream for your attention.

Then say the Lord's Prayer (Matthew 6:9-13). Think about each line, particularly a couple of lines pertinent to work.

Jesus teaches us to say "…Thy Kingdom come, thy will be done, on earth…" We are on earth to build the Kingdom of God. This includes the commercial arena and your workplace. Will God give you the strength and wisdom to bring him to work if you ask for it? Have no doubt that he will.

The Lord's Prayer continues: "Give us this day our daily bread…" This is an important reminder about who provides. God doesn't tell us to provide for ourselves. Jesus asks us to pray that God will provide for us. And we are to ask for our "daily" bread, not this quarter's earnings, or this year's fiscal goal, or sufficient retirement income. We are reminded that life is a day-by-day endeavor. God is not asking us to ignore the future; he is reminding us that each day is a gift. When we remind ourselves that it is God who provides for us each day, the real purpose of work becomes a little more obvious.

Upon saying the Lord's Prayer, ask God to bless those around you at work. If you know a customer who is sick, ask God to heal her. If you know a colleague who is having trouble in his life, ask God to help. Don't limit your prayer to those with identifiable needs; ask God to bless everyone at work – your boss and the company leaders, your colleagues and your subordinates, if you have any. Ask God to bless your customers and your shareholders. Let God define the meaning of those blessings – it may or may not mean financial prosperity.

Include your competitors and even your enemies in your prayer. Again, you don't have to define the nature of the blessings. Simply ask God to bless them and let him determine what form it takes.

When you pray for someone, you inevitably end up being more attuned to him. If you pray for your customers, you likely will end up serving them better. If you pray for your boss or manager, you likely will pay more attention to her. If you pray for your colleagues, you are likely to listen to them more intently. This is an important step for moving into deeper relationship with them. And praying for your enemies is the best way to get rid of them – that is, turn them into tolerable associates, if not friends. It is very difficult to stay mad at people when you are praying for them.

As you close out this prayer during your commute, offer up your day's work to God. Remember that when the Israelites used to make sacrifices to God, they would offer up their best sheep or cattle. They didn't offer up the sick or scrawny animals, they offered up the ones without blemish. So by offering your day's work to God, you are making a commitment to do your best work.

Third, when you are at work, consider setting aside a minute for prayer at one or two specific times during the day. You may even want to set the alarm on your watch to go off at the same time every day as a reminder. Prayer at your desk can be silent so you don't draw attention to yourself. Traditionally, Christians the world over acknowledge noon and three o'clock in the afternoon with prayer. Participation in universal prayer reminds us we are part of something much larger than ourselves.

And fourth, use this small trick to guarantee prayer during your workday if you use a computer: Make your password a prayer. If you get to determine your own computer password, why not make your log-on ritual something spiritual? Use a favorite line from scripture to cobble together a word consisting of the first letter of each word in the verse. For example, if you use John 3:16 "For God so loved the world that he gave his only son…", your password would be FGSLTWTHGHOS. That's a pretty good password. You can make it even more secure by substituting the numeral one for the letter "L" and a zero for the "O."

Prayer is a particularly powerful way to bring God to work because of its three-part impact on the workplace. First, all prayer is some form of conversation between the one who is praying and God. So by praying you enter into a conversation with God, you get to know him better, and you move into deeper relationship with him. Second, your prayer affects those around you. They can be the beneficiary of God's blessing if you pray for them. And third, your prayer can be an effective witness to others about the importance of your faith. Although you should not pray with the idea of attracting attention, it is certainly likely that if you pray at work, over time someone will notice.

Consider ❭ ❭ ❭

1. How serious are you about your prayer life? Do you have established times in your daily schedule for prayer?

2. Has God answered your prayers? Identify specific examples. Is God more likely to give you the answer you seek or something else?

ACTION STEPS ❭ ❭ ❭

1. Start every day with a short prayer of gratitude.

2. Say a prayer on your way to work.

3. Set aside two minutes during the workday for prayer.

For Further Consideration, Read ❭ ❭ ❭

Any book of prayers you find meaningful. A good companion to a prayer book is *The Greatest Thing in the World and Other Essays* by Henry Drummond (Eagle, 1997)

CHAPTER SEVEN

Step Two: Example

"PREACH THE GOSPEL; use words if necessary."

Saint Francis of Assisi is purported to have said that. The statement speaks to the power of example. Actions speak louder than words. We like our leaders to "walk the talk." Certainly those who set an impressive example build incredible personal gravitas. Think about the kinds of people who impress you. Are they folks who say what they are going to do or folks who do what they say?

People will judge you by the example you set, so if you want to bring God to the workplace, your example is important. What kind of example would help to bring God to the workplace?

First, you need to do your job well. If you do sloppy work or you consistently under-perform, you will not win anyone's confidence. When a person does his job well, he builds credibility, which people naturally apply to other areas of life. If you need advice, who do you approach? Do you go to someone who seems to know what he is doing at work or someone who seems clueless and ineffective? Most people choose to go to the competent person, even if they are seeking advice on some matter unrelated to work.

And second, you need to love your neighbor. Loving your neighbor means wanting what's best for them even if it means a little less for you. And, of course, the term "neighbor" includes your colleagues at work.

Jim Johnson, a Lutheran pastor in Southern California, queried people who said they were trying to live their faith at work.[4] "What's the most effective way to bring God to the workplace?" he asked acquaintances in an unscientific survey.

"Live it," said a man who worked for thirty years in a South Dakota technology company. "People won't listen unless you practice your faith. You don't have to be perfect, but genuinely care for people and they will be open to what you say."

"Live as a Christian," said another respondent, a forty-six-year-old Navy contractor in California. "Treat all people as people – from the person dumping the trash to the president of the company."

"Try to show a genuine concern or interest for what is going on in the lives of those around you," said a banker in New York.

"Walk the talk in your daily choices and actions," said a research and development executive with Procter & Gamble. "Instead of talking about being a good Christian, one needs to do it every single day. Others will come to see your inner peace and want to follow."

"Be a living example of God's power and grace," added a forty-three-year-old real estate professional.

One of the best examples is great service. Not everyone works in retail, but everyone has customers. Whoever your customers are, give them superior attention. Whether your customer is solely your boss or hundreds of shoppers at the mall, one of the best ways to show love is to provide service that exceeds their expectations.

There are all kinds of books detailing extraordinary service. Jack Mitchell's book "Hug Your Customers" is filled with examples of employees going the extra mile. Mitchell writes about opening up after hours to help someone buy a tie or a shirt needed for an important meeting. He writes about making special shipping arrangements to get purchases to customers in destinations half-way around the world. One particularly entertaining example has Mitchell buying cowboy hats for a customer, even though Mitchell doesn't typically carry such hats. Mitchell figured out where to get the desired hats and shipped them, to the delight of a new customer.

Great service requires creativity. As Mitchell demonstrates, great service often means figuring out how to do something that's a little bit out of the ordinary. It requires thought and initiative. When you take initiative for someone, you are telling them they are special. You are respecting their human dignity. If you treat people like they are special, you will do a lot to bring God to the workplace, even if you never mention God's name.

You know how you like to be treated; treat those around you that way and you will set a powerful example.

Consider 〉 〉 〉

1. What kind of example are those around you setting? Which examples stand out the most?

2. What kind of example are you setting? Does your example suggest that your faith is important to you?

ACTION STEPS 〉 〉 〉

1. Do something to show your colleagues you love them. Sacrificial, on-going practices (such as permanently trading parking places with someone who has a spot farther away than yours) are better than superficial gestures (like bringing in unwanted leftovers from last night's Super Bowl party).

2. Improve the level of service you offer your customers. If you are unsure about how to do this, ask your boss and colleagues to help you come up with specific actions to take.

For Further Consideration, Read 〉 〉 〉

Hug Your Customers: The Proven Way to Personalize Sales and Achieve Astounding Results by Jack Mitchell (Hyperion, 2003)

CHAPTER EIGHT

Step Three: Conversation

EXAMPLE LEADS TO conversation. People are always watching; some of them will ask you about your actions, particularly if they are unique. Actions that reflect a convicted faith can be unique in the mostly secular commercial world. For example, if you make time to go to church while on a business trip, accompanying colleagues will likely ask about it. This opens the door to conversation about your faith.

Some people make it a point to read scripture during air travel. They don't make a big deal out of it, but many times the person sitting in the next seat sees the Bible and makes a comment. Having shown a spiritual interest, the reader seizes the opportunity to talk to their seatmate about God.

Similar opportunities can come up in the office. Wall-hangings – paintings, posters or photos – can suggest spiritual themes. A Bible in an office bookcase can be an inspiration. People commonly display holy cards, crosses or other religious icons in their cubicle or locker. Even your screensaver can feature a graphic with a religious theme. Like a good example, such displays can invite conversation.

First Peter 3:15 reminds us to "always be ready to give an

explanation to anyone who asks you for a reason for your hope." When someone asks about your faith, they give you an opportunity to bring God into the workplace. It is important to be prepared to make the most of these opportunities. That means you need to know your faith, but even more, it means you need to know how to listen, offer your attention, and respond with grace.

We know how important good communication is. Scripture gives us an example of what happens when people lose the ability to communicate. In Genesis 11, the construction of the tower at Babel grinds to a halt when no one can understand each other. In a converse example presented in Acts 2, the Apostles launch the Christian evangelization initiative when they gain the ability to communicate across language barriers.

Levels of conversational skill, of course, vary. Some people are comfortable talking about anything to anyone. Others struggle. Conversation presents more of an opportunity for some people than others but regardless of your communication skills the workplace opportunity to enter into conversation about your faith is greater than ever. Decades ago, people might not have considered the workplace an appropriate venue for conversations about faith but that has changed at many companies. NBC News poll results released in March 2005 revealed that a majority of people surveyed said religious beliefs play some role in the decisions they make at work, and 65 percent said those beliefs influence how they interact with co-workers.

In an article that the MSNBC web site published about the poll, a faith/culture expert from Yale University said: "Twenty or thirty years ago, there was a sense, particularly in the Northeast, that there were certain topics that just weren't suitable for the work-place: politics, sex and religion. Now we see that people are able to talk about sex very freely, and politics everybody talks about now. It seems like it's almost a logical extension for faith…"[5]

The question in the early twenty-first century American workplace isn't so much "Can I speak about my faith?" but "When should I speak about my faith?" Consider first two instances when you absolutely should speak up.

First, if you find yourself in a situation where people are attacking God or your beliefs, you should stand up for your faith. You don't need to be dramatic about it, but you should make it clear that not everyone in the room goes along with the prevailing conversation. Years ago, a businessman was getting a ride from the airport to his hotel. All of the six passengers in the shuttle were men, traveling to the same industry conference. When talk turned to late night partying, along with crude language about some of the women they hoped would be in attendance, the businessman, who had been listening quietly, interrupted.

"Hey, guys, listen to yourselves," he said. "Every one of us is married. None of us would be talking like this in front of our families. Think about it." That's all he said. The conversation stopped and before too long talk turned to another subject. The businessman didn't mention God, but he spoke up because of his faith in God. When he heard colleagues attacking the lifestyle at the core of his faith, he spoke up. Nobody criticized him for it. In fact, they all agreed with him. All they needed was a little reminder to keep them on track.

Second, if someone asks you about your faith, you need to be ready to respond. Whether someone approaches you with a comment about the faith they see you living, or they ask you a broader moral question, you should make the most of such an opportunity. Don't brush it off. Seriously consider the inquiry and share your thoughts. If someone trusts you enough to approach you with a spiritual question, feel honored, and then offer a thoughtful response.

Beyond these two situations, use your discretion to discern whether it makes sense to share something verbally about your faith. The opportunity is going to vary depending upon your colleagues, company culture and your own demeanor. Consider these guidelines for initiating conversations about your faith at work:

❭ Establish a relationship with a person before introducing the subject of your faith in a conversation.

❭ Don't preach or proselytize. People may be interested in hearing your story but almost no one likes to be told what to believe or do. Your job is to witness; let the Holy Spirit do the converting.

❭ Only bring up faith out of genuine compassion for the colleague or customer, never for your own glory. Your motivation should originate in your heart, not your ego.

❭ Generally, choose peers for this kind of dialogue. Lines of authority make the playing field uneven if you choose to enter into such conversations with subordinates or bosses. If the other party thinks a performance review is in play, they won't be able to listen sincerely or speak freely. This guideline should be broken only if the parties share a well-established, close friendship.

❭ Don't take advantage of a captive audience. Don't turn a scheduled presentation on accounting into a personal witness. People don't like surprises, especially when they can't leave if they don't like it.

Sometimes, a workplace is simply too politically charged for anyone to ever feel sufficiently comfortable to discuss their faith. In those cases, seek a different professional environment away from work to share your faith. Professional associations or trade groups for your industry may present the best opportunity for you to bring God to your occupation. Meetings, seminars and social events sponsored by such groups offer the advantage of pulling together people who share professional interests but don't work in close proximity.

Some companies are large enough that employees from unrelated departments can form groups to meet during lunch or after hours in an environment where faith can freely be discussed.

Churches offer the safest environment for such discussion. Increasingly, churches are creating opportunities for people to discuss the pressures of living their faith in the commercial world. The explosion of the "men's group" movement has expanded the number of spiritual opportunities for men in the workplace. Almost any kind of faith sharing or study group, however, provides an opportunity to discuss your faith in the context of the office or factory.

The Gospel of John opens with the statement that "In the beginning was the Word and the Word was with God and the Word was God." The word is a powerful thing. Our greatest opportunity to connect with others is through the word, spoken in face to face conversation. Of course, many people speak, but few have anything to say. Share the word at work and you will have something to say.

Consider ❱ ❱ ❱

1. Does your example invite conversation about life's deep questions?

2. Have you ever asked a colleague for their thoughts on a moral dilemma or about their faith life?

3. Are you prepared to share your faith, should the opportunity come up? If someone asked what you believe, what would you say?

4. Is the environment in your workplace such that you could have a private conversation with someone to share your faith? If not, could you do anything to change the company environment so that such conversations could take place?

ACTION STEP ❱ ❱ ❱

Share your faith with at least one colleague in the next six months; consider whether that conversation happens best at the workplace or elsewhere.

For Further Consideration, Read ❱ ❱ ❱

Tuesdays with Morrie: an Old Man, a Young Man, and Life's Greatest Lesson by Mitch Albom (Doubleday, 1997)

CHAPTER NINE

Counsel from Matthew

MATTHEW, WHOSE WRITING is presented as the first of the four gospels, knew a lot about business. As a tax collector, he was a businessman. A true entrepreneur, he likely paid the Roman government a fee for the privilege of collecting taxes from those around him. The Romans gave the job to the highest bidder. The shrewdest tax collectors of the time knew who had the most money and how much they could realistically assess against them to cover their own expenses, forward revenue to the government and keep a handsome profit for themselves.

Matthew would have had a good grasp of business practices in a variety of trades. He would have come into contact with people who were successful in business and those who struggled. He would have seen up close what works in business and what doesn't.

It should come as no surprise that Matthew's Gospel is filled with stories that apply to business settings. The GEO Principle finds five stories relayed by Matthew to be particularly instructive for people in the workplace, even some two thousand years after they were recorded.

Do what you say you are going to do

Matthew 21:28-31

A father asks his two sons to work in the vineyard; one says he will work and never does, the other says he won't work but changes his mind and ultimately does. The focus of the story usually is on the one who decides to go after initially saying he won't. He is the one who does his father's will. But think about the one who lies and doesn't go to work. Jesus says prostitutes will go to heaven before this kind of person. Wow! If you say you are going to do something, you need to do it. Or if you have no intention of doing something, don't say you will. The meaning of words needs to be respected; if you make a promise to a colleague, a boss, a vendor or a customer, keep it!

In this story, one son under-promises and over-delivers; the other son over-promises and under-delivers. The story offers a valuable business lesson. It is better to promise less and deliver more; people who consistently promise a lot and deliver little don't hold much credibility in the work world. Nobody likes a big talker; we like big doers. Sometimes, it is better to just do something rather than to talk about it.

We don't know whether the son who didn't go to work changed his mind after giving his word or whether he never intended to go in the first place. If he changed his mind, he should have told his father. Anyone can appreciate the fact that, inevitably, things come up that sometimes prevent people from keeping their word. But nobody likes to be stood up. So if you suddenly realize you can't live up to a promise, communicate to the affected people. Then come up with an alternative for living up to the original commitment.

Do your homework

Matthew 21:23-27

In this story, the chief priests of the temple attempt to trap Jesus by asking him to name the authority under which he acts. Christ responds with his own question about whether John the Baptist was of heavenly or human origin. The chief priests are unable to answer and Jesus, therefore, dismisses them.

The story provides a couple of lessons. First, questions should be asked sincerely. Those chief priests didn't care what Jesus would answer; they were insincere. They did not respect him and were only trying to trap him. But Jesus ends up embarrassing them. This is often what happens when people ask questions in an attempt to trap someone. A questioner should be genuinely interested in what the respondent has to say. No one should assume they already know the answer; don't solicit an answer with the intention of using it against the respondent.

Second, this story shows the importance of good preparation. Anyone who poses a question to someone important better know what they are talking about. Jesus dismissed the chief priests' question because they obviously were not prepared to have a meaningful conversation. When you approach a colleague, a boss, a vendor or a customer, make sure you are ready to have a meaningful conversation. Be prepared. Never pretend to know something you don't; eventually, you'll only embarrass yourself.

Resolve disputes with dignity

Matthew 18:15-17

Managing is easy when everything is going well; the real test of managerial skill comes when there are problems. Matthew provides a sound blueprint for confronting problems caused by other individuals. If an employee causes a problem, go to him or her quietly and try to work it out between the two of you. If that effort fails, then bring along a witness or someone else knowledgeable about the situation. With the additional person, you should be able to make a stronger case; the two of you may be able to persuade the person causing the trouble. If not, then you need to bring the matter before an organized body that can offer ethical guidance. This could be a professional association of peers. If even this step fails, then take the matter to the courts.

This model is admirable because it respects the dignity of both the individual at the center of the problem and the dignity of the general public. By attempting to resolve the situation privately, a boss shows respect for the individual. By reserving the courts for worst-case scenarios, the public is relieved of work and expense associated with problems that can be addressed on a more local level.

This is also an important model for dealing with delinquent customers. If someone falls behind on a payment, seek him out individually to discuss the situation. Make sure you understand their situation; give them a chance to work something out with you before initiating legal procedures. Delinquent customers should be contacted in person or by telephone before services are terminated or before any notices are filed that will permanently mar the customer's credit record.

Think outside the box
Matthew 18:21-22

When Peter asks Jesus if it is enough to forgive a sinner seven times, he thinks he is being generous. Jesus responds with an answer no one would have come up with – seventy times seven times! It's a large, outside-the-box number. Jesus clearly is not in favor of the status quo. He sets a new standard. Jesus raises the bar to a level no one ever considered realistic.

We should be as bold as Jesus. Don't be afraid to think about typical situations in new ways. That means, don't accept status quo as the only way to do things; look for exponentially better ways to do things. Don't be afraid to set the bar ridiculously high. Look for answers in unconventional places. Operate with the idea that everything is on the table. Don't get boxed into tradition and convention when it comes to addressing challenges at work. Maybe it's not a matter of coming up with a better mousetrap but of deciding to go after a different kind of animal. Think big; be bold. Christ is our model.

Be prepared to live with unscrupulous competitors
Matthew 13:24-30

In this parable, the master doesn't allow the laborers to pull up the weeds because they might accidentally pull up the wheat as well. In the modern commercial world, just like in this story, the wheat and the weeds are growing up together. There are all kinds of people and companies, including some who don't play by the rules. Everyone knows people who cheat and companies that follow questionable practices.

It would be nice to think that whenever someone did something wrong, justice would instantly be administered and fairness re-established. This might be envisioned in the form of a lightening bolt striking the bad guys when they lie or steal or cheat. But, of course, that doesn't happen. This parable tells us it won't.

The fact is, the world will always be filled with people who do good and people who do bad; we all have to get through life together. Fortunately, we are not literally wheat and weeds. While weeds cannot change into wheat, people can change. People can reverse their own patterns of ill behavior. And your good example just might help them to do so.

Consider ❭ ❭ ❭

1. Are you implementing any business practices that could be considered misleading or deceptive?

2. When you make a commitment, do you go the extra mile to live up to that commitment, even if it's not the subject of a written contract?

3. Do you respect your clients, prospects, colleagues and others enough to sufficiently prepare for meetings with them?

4. Do you look for new ways to do things? Have you ever tried something unconventional at work? Did it succeed? If not, is that failure keeping you from continuing to look for better ways to practice your business?

5. Can you see how your work is affecting your relationship with God? Is it helping you move closer to him or is it distancing you from him?

6. How do you deal with delinquent customers?

7. Do you have competitors who don't play by the rules? How much energy do you spend focusing on the disparity? Could that energy be better spent?

ACTION STEPS 〉 〉 〉

1. Read the entire Book of Matthew. Consider his instruction in the light of his profession as a tax collector and entrepreneur.

2. Identify a half dozen scripture passages that you believe offer a message about how to act in the commercial world. Record your thoughts so you can easily recall them when applicable situations arise at work.

For Further Consideration, Read 〉 〉 〉

The Gospels of Mark and Luke

CHAPTER TEN

But I Can't
Bring God to *this* Job!

MANY PEOPLE AVOID the very notion of bringing God to work because they hate their job. Or if they don't outright hate it, they think it is somehow unworthy of God. They say things like, "My job is boring," or "my colleagues are hostile," or "no one else there is a believer." Over time, people have come up with hundreds of reason to leave God at home, like that forgotten lunch pail on the kitchen table.

Granted, there are some places where it is not only difficult to bring God to work, but where the work itself is so contrary to God's will that you need to get out of there fast. If you work for the "Sopranos," or you are a bouncer in a strip club, or you work in some kind of high-pressure sales scam, you have a problem. Recall the first family – Joseph, Mary and Jesus. When Herod made the environment in Bethlehem hostile to Jesus by ordering the death of every baby boy in the area, Joseph hustled out of there, not only to protect his child and Mary, but to protect himself. In the same way, if you are in an environment hostile to God, you need to hustle out of there. If you work at a business that produces pornographic movies, for example, then you need to find another job. You endanger your own soul by remaining, and your chances of pointing others toward God in such an environment are slim.

If you are trying to decide whether you work in one of those places, be sure to distinguish between the veneer of the people doing the work and the actual work that is being done. The latter is far more important. For example, congenial people working a scam to steal credit card numbers create a dire working environment, whereas foul-mouthed laborers only make a construction site uncomfortable. Specific tasks can be judged objectively to be honorable or dishonorable, while people can change, making judgment much more difficult. If the work is honorable but the people are disagreeable, give the people the benefit of the doubt; whereas if the work is dishonorable, get out of there as fast as you can even if your colleagues are collegial.

Often, when people think about integrating their faith with their work, they decide they need to work in a non-profit environment. They think they should work for a charity or church organization. People sometimes have trouble seeing lasting purpose in public relations work, the legal field, financial services, transportation or whatever their current line of work.

To be sure, some people are called to work in the non-profit sector. But most are not. The for-profit sector is supposed to be larger than the non-profit sector. Most people work in for-profit settings entirely inviting to God's presence. Profit is a good thing. As Joseph mentored a young Jesus, one assumes he ran a profitable carpentry business.

Whether an organization is set up as a for-profit enterprise or a non-profit organization, the people working there define the work environment. The fact is, the same office politics that infect some businesses are alive and well in some church offices. People are people, no matter where they work.

More important than distinctions between for-profit and non-profit organizations may be ownership distinctions among for-profit businesses. Investors buy shares in publicly held companies solely for the purpose of making money. Absent the expectations of outside investors, owners of closely held businesses can have motives in addition to profit, such as a desire to help certain employees, an inclination to stimulate a local economy, or loyalty to a special customer group. Owners of privately-held businesses are free to make accommodations that negatively affect earnings in the short term, a freedom that managers at publicly held companies simply don't have. The typically superior compensation and benefits of public company employment should be weighed against the increased flexibility of the private company environment. No business, of course, can survive too long without sufficient earnings, but privately held businesses have a little more flexibility than public companies, depending on the disposition of their owners.

Because most workplaces are perfectly suited for God – at least as well as that stable in Bethlehem – most people don't need to change jobs to integrate their faith with their work. For the majority, the GEO Principle does not mean changing jobs.

God-fearing people, to clarify, are not pushovers to obnoxious employers; the GEO Principle does not mean accepting any job or working arrangement. Considerations such as the extent to which your interests match your career path, compensation, location, schedule and security may indicate a change is in order, but these considerations are independent of any effort to bring God to work.

Integrating your faith and work is not so much about finding meaningful work as it is about making work meaningful. The site of the nativity was a perfectly fine stable, but it didn't become a meaningful place until after Mary and Joseph brought God there. People who bring God to the job they already have are likely to find meaning in their work long before the job jumper who leaves God at home.

Whatever your job, your ability to consider that job in a larger context can have a huge impact on work fulfillment. It is important to understand the role that job plays in the department, in the company, in the industry, in the marketplace and in the culture.

Consider the man who walks up to a construction site and sees three plumbers, each fitting pieces of copper piping together. He asks, "What are you doing?"

"I am installing some pipes," answers the first plumber.

"I'm putting in a heating system," answers the second plumber.

"I'm building a house," answers the third plumber.

All three are doing the same thing but each sees his work differently. Which plumber do you think derives the most satisfaction from his work? If you want any measure of fulfillment from your work, you want to be like the third plumber. Any good company tries to communicate to employees the "big picture," but ultimately it is up to the employee to seek the breadth of information necessary to see his own work in context.

Sadly, some employers deliberately keep their employees needlessly in the dark about the scope of their work. But it is even sadder when employees choose to work in the dark. Although minimal work engagement might seem appealing in the short term, it offers no prospect for long-term work satisfaction. Learn all you can about your work and its impact on the world.

Surveys commonly report that a substantial portion of the workforce dislikes their jobs, and certainly there are plenty of unpleasant jobs out there. Maybe you are doing one of them. But how many of those people who are unhappy in their job would be unhappy in *any* job? Probably a large percentage of them. If you are serious about your work, the best way to find meaning in it is to bring that meaning to work yourself. Don't leave God at home, hoping someone else will bring him to your workplace. Bring him to work yourself. Your example might inspire your colleagues to follow suit.

Consider ❱ ❱ ❱

1. What is your attitude about your job? What factors contribute to that attitude?

2. How well do you understand the context of your work? What is its impact on your office, company, community, country and our world?

ACTION STEPS ❱ ❱ ❱

1. Learn something new about your industry in order to deepen your understanding of the context of your work.

2. Develop a two- or three-sentence statement that articulates the work you do and its role in our world.

For Further Consideration, Read ❱ ❱ ❱

The 7 Habits of Highly Effective People: Powerful Lessons in Personal Change by Stephen Covey (Fireside Books, Simon & Schuster 1990)

CHAPTER ELEVEN

Faith Prepares Us for Change

JOB CHANGE, EVEN if it isn't necessary to protect your soul, can still be worth pondering in the context of your willingness to bring God to work. But rather than looking at the work, look at yourself. Do you like who you are in your job?

It is an important question because finding the right fit in a job is more about who you *are* than about what you *do*. Jesus transformed the stable because of who he was, not because of what he did. This is the model for us in the workplace – not to diminish the importance of what you do, but to augment the importance of who you are. In order to bring God to work, you need to be humble, competent and flexible.

Pride sometimes leads people into thinking they need to change jobs. Everyone thinks they deserve better; everyone thinks they should be paid more. A certain amount of humility, therefore, is necessary to honestly consider whether a job is right. Set aside, for a moment, what you do and think about what you are: Are you humble?

In "Good to Great," author Jim Collins looks at characteristics of successful CEOs and discovers that humility is essential. In one of the most popular business books ever written, Collins writes: "The best leaders display a compelling modesty, are self-effacing and understated. They are humble." The best CEOs are not braggarts, Collins says. They attribute success to other people but when things go wrong, they take responsibility.[6]

Humility doesn't mean walking around with your head down, responding "ah shucks" whenever anyone asks something. Being humble means admitting you don't know everything. Collins is saying those really successful CEOs are willing to listen to others. Collins assures that no matter where you are in your career, you can benefit from listening to others. And that starts with humility.

No one who knows scripture should be surprised by Collin's conclusion. "Conduct your affairs with humility and you will be loved more than a giver of gifts. Humble yourself the more, the greater you are, and you will find favor with God. For great is the power of God; by the humble he is glorified." This passage is from the third chapter of Sirach (17-19). Or consider this passage from Proverbs (22:4): "The reward of humility and fear of the Lord is riches, honor and life."

Do you have trouble being humble? Humility does not come easily to most people. One of the best strategies for cultivating humility is gratitude. Take time every day to count your blessings. The more you thank God for what you have, the more you realize you don't deserve it. God is so generous. The more you understand God's generosity, the more humble you naturally become.

As you further consider whether your job is a good fit, honestly evaluate your skills and expertise. Are you competent? It is important that you are good at the work you do, relative to the amount of experience you have. In chapter seven, we noted the importance of professional competence. People naturally look to competent colleagues for insight and leadership. And they will look to those people for answers about important subjects unrelated to work. Many people conclude that if someone has his professional life together, he must have his personal life figured out too. This may or may not be a fair conclusion, but it is a common one.

And finally, as you consider whether you are in the right job, consider your adaptability. Are you flexible? Many people expect things to stay the same, for at least as long as they are working there. But the fact is, things change. The world, especially the work world, is a dynamic place. Tom Peters called it chaos.

Christians, however, have somewhat of an edge. John the Baptist, in preparing the way for the Lord, called on people to "repent." That means he challenged people to change. Those who chose to follow Christ did change. Following Christ always means leaving behind old, selfish ways. It requires a change that turns us toward God. Oftentimes, the change is not easy. The glamour of the old ways can be alluring. People willing to amend their lives for God have valuable experience with change. This kind of experience should make it easier to manage less significant change, like shifts in the workplace. Companies are bought and sold, jobs get altered, responsibilities get reassigned, and the view up the corporate ladder fogs. These are significant changes at work but they are minor compared to the kind of repentant change necessary to follow God.

As you consider whether you are in the right job, think about what you do, but think more intently about who you are. Are you humble, competent and flexible? Work on who you are, and it will be easier to manage what you do.

If you decide you want to convert thoughts about changing jobs to action, consider Paul as an example. Recall the story in Acts of the Apostles where Paul is involved in a shipwreck. Washing up on the shores of Malta, scripture tells us Paul "gathered a bundle of sticks and laid them on the fire…" (Acts 28:3). It was a situation where Paul simply looked around and did what needed to be done. He did something he was suited for. He didn't try to repair the boat; he made a fire. He didn't wait for someone to tell him to make a fire. He looked for something to do and did it.

Acts of the Apostles wasn't written as a job-hunter's guide but Paul's example is powerful advice: *Don't wait for someone to tell you what to do; look around and figure out what needs to be done. Then do it.*

If you want a different job, look around and figure out what needs to be done. If you look around your office, city or country you will discover lots of things that need to be done, lots of problems that need solving. Devise a way to fulfill any one of the needs you identify and you will have significant work. An actual job opening somewhere might address the need you identify, but it is more likely there won't be an opening addressing the specific need you see. It may be up to you to map out a strategy for a new business line, take your plan to a company positioned to sponsor that business, and pitch your idea to the person in charge. Your initiative will reflect well on you. If your idea is sufficiently compelling, a good business owner will create a job for you, especially if you've included a way to share or mitigate the business risk. If no one will listen, then you might need to go directly to the market. Figure out a way to offer the service or create the product on your own.

While sole proprietorship, entrepreneurship and small business ventures have offered reward for years, the early twenty-first century makes this career arena more viable than ever. Not everyone is meant to run their own company but far more people today realistically have this option than ever before in modern times. People who are contemplating job or career change cannot afford to ignore entrepreneurial avenues. In his book "The World is Flat," Thomas Friedman describes an incredible world in which the smallest players can now compete with long-established, corporate giants. Developments such as Voice Over Internet Protocol, UPS logistics support, Google and email have leveled the business playing field. Anyone with internet access has low-cost advertising opportunities if they maximize the social network like YouTube, Blogger and PRweb.com. An individual working out of a basement on a shoestring budget can now handle business responsibilities that would have required dozens of people in the 1980s.

Granted, even with twenty-first century advantages, most people prefer a job with an established company. Regardless of whether you intend to apply for a job or create your own, job seekers can get an edge if they focus on problem solving. People who are willing to look around, identify problems and fix them will always be employable.

Change is rarely easy but faith-filled people should know a thing or two about change. Throughout Jesus' public ministry, he called on people to change. He challenged the apostles to leave their boats and follow him. He asked the woman about to be stoned to sin no more. He is calling all of us to leave our old ways behind.

Change is a big part of the work world. Companies go out of business. One company buys another, people lose their jobs. Or some new invention comes along and completely changes the business. As long as the world is full of thinking, active people, the world is going to change. Knowledge is going to grow and with that additional knowledge, people are going to figure out new ways to do things.

Think, for example, of how the internet has changed the job market. Consider the travel agents who lost their jobs when everyone started using online reservation services. Or think about all the people in the newsroom who were laid off when newspaper design went computerized. Or think about the many Americans who are losing jobs as their work is being outsourced to India or Malaysia. Change has been taking place for centuries and it won't stop. Think of the candle makers who lost jobs when the light bulb was invented. Or consider the blacksmith, who probably had a pretty good thing going until the automobile came along.

Don't be surprised when change arrives, and don't expect it to knock politely at your door. Use change as an opportunity to re-evaluate your life, to think about where you are, and to consider how your work is helping you to grow closer to God.

Consider ❭ ❭ ❭

1. Are you humble, competent and flexible? Can you think of examples to justify your answer?

2. If you had to start your own company, what would you do and how would you do it?

3. In your life, is change typically thrust upon you or do you initiate it?

ACTION STEPS ❭ ❭ ❭

1. Identify at least three specific problems or challenges at work. Come up with a plan for resolving them and implement the plan.

2. Identify someone who has been adversely affected by a job-place change. Help him or her deal with the change, perhaps even assisting in a job search.

For Further Consideration, Read ❭ ❭ ❭

Good to Great: Why Some Companies Make the Leap…and Others Don't by Jim Collins (HarperCollins Publishing, Inc., 2001)

Chapter Twelve

Lifespan

CENTURIES AGO, PEOPLE planned to work their whole lives and those who practiced their faith knew that at the end of life, death would usher in a new phase – ultimate happiness with their Maker in heaven. Something happened in the nineteenth and twentieth centuries in America, however, that substantially altered such thinking. The idea of working at a sustainable pace for a lifetime with an eternal reward in heaven was replaced by the notion of working at burnout pace for a few decades, followed by a more immediate reward, a period of leisure called retirement. The role of heaven, and the prerequisite relationship with God, was moved out of the picture.

Although retirement in the United States is largely a post World War II notion, most Americans today can hardly imagine life without it. Just about every American assumes the last third of life should be set aside for full-time leisure. A multi-billion dollar investment industry was built on the efforts of millions of Americans saving their money for those golden retirement years. As the typical lifespan lengthened during the twentieth century, the cultural expectations grew clear: those additional years should be devoted to golf, travel or other forms of relaxation.

The trimester view of lifespan consists of youth, adulthood and the golden years. The first segment, which typically runs through age twenty-three or so, is dedicated to education. The second segment, from the mid twenties to the mid sixties, is devoted to work. And the third segment, commencing at retirement, is devoted to leisure. By studying longer and retiring sooner, many people find ways to reduce the amount of time devoted to the work phase. For this growing group of people, each life phase represents about the same number of years.

The modern approach to lifespan can be illustrated as follows, with life's journey taking a person from birth, through each trimester, to death. People typically view the trimesters above the timeline to be positive experiences, while the work trimester, illustrated below the timeline, is usually viewed negatively.

LIFESPAN: CONVENTIONAL VIEW

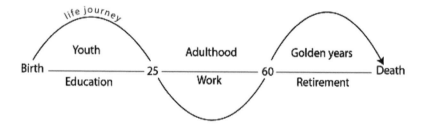

The GEO Principle, however, invites you to something better. The GEO Principle considers lifespan in the context of a relationship with God. Rather than seeing life as a series of three successive phases, each trimester replacing the previous one, the GEO

Principle considers lifespan along an eternal timeline made up of concurrent components: play, learning, worship and work. Rather than considering your life from the perspective of your body, starting at birth and ending at death, think of it from the perspective of your soul, starting with conception and never ending. Picture it like this:

LIFESPAN: GEO PRINCIPLE VIEW

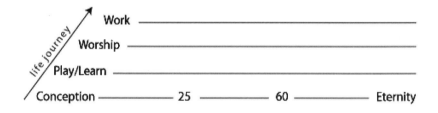

Contrast this illustration of lifespan with the conventional one. Note the direction the GEO Principle approach sets for the life journey – up, toward God.

Let's look more closely at each component of the GEO Principle lifespan view.

Consider ❱ ❱ ❱

1. Do you see your life easily described by the conventional, trimester view of lifespan?

2. Are you counting down the years (days) until retirement? Why?

ACTION STEP ❱ ❱ ❱

Using pen and paper, create a timeline for your life, recording major events according to approximate dates. Include at least four milestones, including those related to your faith, for every decade of your life. Do any patterns emerge?

For Further Consideration, Read ❱ ❱ ❱

Our Town by Thornton Wilder (Harper & Row, 1938)

CHAPTER THIRTEEN

Start with Play

FROM THE TIME you were in your mother's womb, you were playing. A pre-born child may kick or pull on its toes. An infant shakes a rattle. A child throws a ball or runs with neighbors. As people mature, play remains important. High school kids play sports, and college students socialize late into the night. Adults enjoy their fishing gear, golf clubs and frequent flyer miles. Senior citizens play as much or more than anyone. Magazines published by AARP are filled with pictures of white-haired people river rafting, biking and hiking.

Scientists, indeed, are finding that play is an essential component to healthy living, for kids and adults. Dr. Stuart Brown, the founder of the National Institute for Play, says "humans are uniquely designed by nature to enjoy and participate in play throughout life."

Dr. Brown spent a career cataloguing play profiles of thousands of people. His conclusion: "Play is important in the accomplishments of successful people, and negative consequences inevitably accumulate in the lives of play-deprived people." He says "play is as basic and pervasive a natural phenomenon as sleep." Dr. Brown maintains that play refreshes relationships, fosters learning, increases one's capacity for appreciating humor, boosts creativity and results in a host of other positives.[7]

Although science is quantifying the benefits of play, people know of those benefits instinctively. Most adults crave playtime or leisure as much as they crave fresh air and clean water. People in some corners of the commercial arena have successfully integrated play into their professional routine. Many salespeople, for example, entertain prospects on the golf course. Other business people entertain on boats or in box seats at the ballgame.

But you don't have to leave the office to find a playful, inspiring environment. Some offices make space for pool tables or even basketball courts. One of the more interesting professional spaces in suburban Minneapolis is the "think tank" at a consulting firm called The Prouty Project. The purple, circular room is a glorified conference room featuring floor-to-ceiling whiteboards for writing and drawing. A round table featuring multi-colored inlays accommodates twelve. There are stuffed animals for hugging, stress balls for squeezing and tossing, sunglasses and bells. There are inspirational quotes on the walls, and dictionaries and thesauruses within easy reach so clients can write their own. Jeff Prouty, who runs the place, said the room is an incubator for creative thinking. Countless strategic plans have been birthed in this room, which looks more like a fun house than a corporate board room.

"The practices that organizations need to be developing for their increasingly complex information work are those which infuse the state of play into their workers' attitudes," Dr. Brown writes. "They need to learn how to do the work of their organizations in a play state." The National Institute for Play offers consultative services to companies seeking to incorporate play into their operations.

Many people will find it impractical to incorporate play in their work routines, making hobbies and recreational activities during evening and weekend hours all the more important.

Fortunately, ample athletic opportunities exist, from volleyball to dodgeball. The value of exercise for those who sit at a desk all day is indisputable. Anyone who travels frequently knows the benefit of a good work-out room at the hotel. Bicycling, ballroom dance and other activities which require movement of your entire body are effective tonics.

Play is a lifelong endeavor that enhances a person's ability to learn, worship and work. No matter how you look at lifespan, it would be entirely drudgery without any play. Adults tend to take ourselves seriously, but we should be humble enough to admit we need playtime as well. Play actually strengthens our ability to be serious when we need to be. Drudgery diminishes joy and hope.

Consider ❱ ❱ ❱

1. How much time do you have for play?

2. Do your work time and play time intersect?

ACTION STEP ❱ ❱ ❱

Start a recreational hobby. If you already have one, recommit yourself to it so you are out playing at least three times per month.

For Further Consideration, Read ❱ ❱ ❱

Play: How it Shapes the Brain, Opens the Imagination, and Stimulates the Soul by Stuart Brown, (Avery, 2009)

CHAPTER FOURTEEN

Learning Goes with Play

ALTHOUGH PLAY IS generally associated with youngsters and learning is typically associated with students, play and learning are, in fact, inseparable, lifelong endeavors. Play does not stop when a person begins school. And learning does not stop when a person graduates from college. At all stages of life, it is important to play and learn.

Given how rapidly things change in this world, anyone who hopes to maintain relevant marketplace skills must be prepared to constantly learn. William Carden, a former dean at Texas Tech University, raised this point in a speech he delivered to a business group in the spring of 2005. "There is a knowledge explosion," he said. "Years ago, they used to say that knowledge was doubling every twenty years. Now, about every five years, knowledge is doubling. Two and a half years after someone graduates from college, half of what they were taught will be obsolete."[8]

The old concept of education limited it to something that happened at school, between kindergarten roundup and college graduation. In the middle of the twentieth century, a person could be effective in the workplace with a notion of education that confined learning to the early years of life. But no longer.

"Education can and must go on everywhere all the time – in schools, offices, at home, online, in the classroom, over your iPod – with conventional teachers, self-teaching methods, online games, whatever works. You cannot let up, because somewhere out there there's a competitor who isn't letting up."[9] Those are the words of Thomas Friedman making the case for lifelong learning in "The World is Flat." He says the most important thing we can do is "learn how to learn." He encourages his reader to "constantly absorb, and teach yourself new ways of doing old things or new ways of doing new things. This is an ability every worker should cultivate in an age when parts or all of many jobs are constantly going to be exposed to digitization, automation, and outsourced, and where new jobs, and whole new industries, will be churned up faster and faster."[10]

Fortunately, the opportunities to learn are limitless. Specialized computer training makes it possible for anyone with internet access to study virtually anything. Colleges and universities have all kinds of continuing education programs, in addition to their traditional degree programs. Many cities offer some form of a community education program. Perhaps the greatest, if not most traditional, educational opportunity is the public library, where anyone can borrow virtually any book that's ever been printed. Even more dramatic to learning is search engine technology that puts information right at your fingertips. Want to know…anything? Google it!

Commercial enterprises typically value knowledge. That's why many companies are willing to pay for employees to attend college or undertake additional training. An employer wants its employees' best work. So does the marketplace. Neither readily makes accommodation for people unwilling to keep their skills sharp.

Consider ❱ ❱ ❱

1. Do you consider yourself to be done with education?

2. How do you typically absorb new information: newspaper, radio, television, seminars, formal classes or computer? Is this information merely for entertainment (following a local sports team) or for personal development (studying a foreign language)?

3. What additional knowledge would improve your life?

4. What impact would continuing education have on your life, both at home and at work?

ACTION STEPS ❱ ❱ ❱

1. Explore a new educational opportunity.

2. Set a personal goal of mastering a new area of knowledge or a new skill within one year.

For Further Consideration, Read ❱ ❱ ❱

The World Is Flat: A Brief History of the Twenty-first Century, Updated and Expanded, by Thomas Friedman (Farrar, Straus and Giroux, 2005) Read chapters seven, eight and nine.

CHAPTER FIFTEEN

Add Worship During Childhood

IF A CHILD is fortunate enough to be born into a faith-filled home, it shouldn't be long before the child is exposed to the next lifespan component – worship. This component does not replace play or learning, it complements and fulfills. People of some faith traditions baptize infants, others wait until the person is older. Parents bring their children to church services or liturgy. Some services offer child-appropriate scripture readings and teaching. Catholics confer the sacraments of reconciliation and communion on children at about age seven. Christian teens are confirmed, while Jewish teens celebrate a bar mitzvah or bat mitzvah.

Worship is as fundamental as play and learning. All human beings have a deep-seated yearning to know their Maker. Regardless of whether they were born into a religious family, at some point people ask themselves "Why am I here?" and "What am I supposed to do?" Those are questions about our relationship with God; the answer includes worship. What could be more natural than the created worshipping the Creator?

And while perhaps the most obvious examples of worship happen in church buildings, worship is really about living a right relationship with God. We worship God by living the way he wants us to live, including at work. We can spend a lot of time contemplating exactly what God wants from us, but the basics aren't complicated: Follow the commandments, read the scriptures, reach out to the poor, love your neighbor.

Gratitude is an important form of worship. When you thank God for something, you are worshipping him. A "thank you" acknowledges God as the giver. Every November, we Americans set aside one day specifically to give thanks. Never forget to whom we are giving thanks. It is to God.

In business, the value of saying "thank you" is undisputed. A job candidate who fails to send a thank you note to an interviewer reduces his chances of landing the job. Companies commonly send gifts to valued clients as a way of saying "thanks for the business." And every year at Christmas time, businesses exchange millions of cards that express gratitude for the past year's affiliation.

Just as thanking a client is a way of solidifying a relationship, thanking God is a way to improve our relationship with him. Even though no one could ever thank God sufficiently, that doesn't mean you shouldn't try. Name the greatest blessings in your life: spouse, relatives, friends, health, home, education, work – and don't forget faith itself. You can't go wrong recalling these blessings each day. By thanking God for the things you have, you shift your mind away from the things you don't have. Gratitude helps a person avoid envy, jealousy and other corrosive attitudes.

Gratitude mitigates the effects of want, tempering it against the possibility of becoming greed. Gratitude is your most powerful weapon for combating the unrealistic, have-it-all currents running through the contemporary culture. Gratitude is the antidote to excessive want, sometimes called greed, a particularly alluring temptation in some workplaces. At home or work, excessive want makes fulfillment of any kind impossible.

The flip side of gratitude is self-sacrifice. Clearly, you give up a little when you acknowledge that you have enough. If you restrain yourself from going for the bigger house or the faster car, you are giving those things up. This kind of sacrifice hurts, if even only a little bit. Small, ongoing self-sacrifice prepares a person to handle bigger sacrifices, which inevitably surface in life.

Many religious traditions include a self-sacrifice component. Muslims fast during Ramadan. Jews fast on Yom Kippur. And during Lent, Christians follow Christ's example in the desert, where he fasted. Voluntary, minor sacrifices prepare a person to accept more substantial, involuntary sacrifices, such as job loss, illness, death of a loved one or other hardship. An unexpected setback hits people a lot harder if they are accustomed to getting everything they want, whenever they want it.

Worship, including healthy doses of gratitude and self-sacrifice, naturally complements play, learning and work in the GEO Principle view of lifespan.

Consider ❱ ❱ ❱

1. How old were you when your relationship with God began to mean something to you?

2. Are you in the habit of saying thank you? Are you living an attitude of gratitude?

3. How do you worship God?

4. How are you teaching your children, nieces or nephews to worship God?

5. Have you ever thought about making minor sacrifices in preparation for bigger hardships?

ACTION STEPS ❱ ❱ ❱

1. Take your personal and public/communal worship of God to the next level.

2. Identify someone who you believe may have a tepid relationship with God; invite that person to join you in worship.

For Further Consideration, Read ❱ ❱ ❱

The Book of Job

CHAPTER SIXTEEN

Growing Up:
It's Time to Work

WORK, THE FOURTH lifespan component, naturally flows out of a desire to worship God. For a small number of people that will mean professions in the church, work in a non-profit organization, or dedication to the human services field. But for the vast majority of people, the work God is calling us to perform needs to happen in the commercial arena – stock brokerage firms, construction companies, media, accounting practices, factories, restaurants, department stores, or on airplanes, trains or ships.

People generally begin careers in their twenties but the value of earlier work should not be discounted. Jobs at a burger joint, movie theater or amusement park provide important training to teens and college kids. For many people who work during their high school and college years, entry into the workforce is a gradual process that takes years. Those early years offer an important opportunity to learn about time management, teamwork, organizational structure, wages and taxes, and customer expectations.

By a person's mid or late twenties, work begins to complement the earlier-established lifespan components of play, learning and worship. Play now helps a person sustain a viable work pace;

commercial application of knowledge typically adds value to the enterprise; and work offers a person a whole new arena in which to witness and develop a relationship with God. Work does not replace play, learning or worship, but brings them fuller meaning.

Work is how we co-create with God. We enter into deeper relationship with him by working at God's side, whether that's in the bargain basement of the store or the fortieth floor of a skyscraper. When we make a widget, build a car, assemble a computer, produce a document or create in some other fashion, we are co-creating with God. Early in a career it is easy to think that we do these things on our own, but as we develop our relationship with God at work, it becomes evident just how small a role we have in it all.

The modern-day notion of retirement doesn't mean much to people living a rich relationship with God through the execution of professional duties in the workplace. The sudden cessation of work, at the predetermined age of sixty-five, makes little sense. The natural aging of the human body will dictate a gradual winding down of professional activities, but for many people that time will come far later than the traditional retirement date.

Everyone dies, but faith-filled people do not believe death is the end of their life. People who are right with God will know eternity in heaven, and the GEO Principle contends that the work/faith relationship will continue to be important. In heaven, there will be important work to do. As long as there are people on the planet, those in heaven will pray for those on Earth. While it is no longer necessary for those in heaven to pray for themselves, they know folks on Earth need prayers. This intercessory prayer is work that is as serious as anything anyone is doing right now on Earth.

Earthly work takes on substantially more meaning if we view the work/faith relationship as eternal. Track coaches often instruct their long-distance runners to imagine the finish line to be about 25 yards beyond the actual end of the course. Coaches understand the natural inclination people have to slow down before the finish line, to stop before the job is done.

Paul, the great evangelist, compared life to a race (2 Timothy 4:7, 1 Corinthians 9:24). Death is not the end of the work/faith relationship. We need to resist the natural tendency to quit before the race is over. The marathon of life carries us through death, after which we will cheer for those still running. In the meantime, while still on Earth, play, learning and worship prepare us to make the most of work in a life-long journey toward our Maker.

Consider ❱ ❱ ❱

1. Would you be content to work the remainder of your life?

2. When you think about your future, do you typically include the afterlife?

ACTION STEP ❱ ❱ ❱

Reconsider the timeline you created at the end of chapter twelve. Is your life a series of unrelated, successive events, or is it a deepening relationship with God where events build upon one another to strengthen your faith and character?

For Further Consideration, Read ❱ ❱ ❱

On Human Work by Pope John Paul II, (September 1981) Start with Section II.

CHAPTER SEVENTEEN

Honor the Sabbath

GOD MADE THE world in six days and then he took a day off – not because he needed to, but in order to set an example for us about work. Rest is important.

Animals work all the time. They don't know whether it's Monday or Sunday. But people do know the difference and God even gave us a commandment so that we wouldn't forget. We are commanded to keep holy the Sabbath. You might wonder how to do that; the GEO Principle starts with the example God gave us in the first pages of the Bible.

Work, however, can be seductive. "We have to guard ourselves…from the dangers of excessive activity, regardless of the office one holds, because too many concerns can often lead to hardness of heart. This warning is valid for every type of job," Pope Benedict XVI cautioned.[11] In our get-ahead culture, it is easy to let a forty-hour work week grow into a fifty-hour work week. "Oh, I'll just go in an hour early every day and leave an hour late," you tell yourself. Then it grows to fifty-five hours a week. "I'll start coming in on Saturdays." And then it becomes a sixty-hour-plus work week. "I really need to come in on Sundays to get all my work done."

If your workload increases, think about working smarter, not longer. Set time aside to plan your work. Determine whether there are things you can drop from your to-do list. Do you really need to attend that meeting? Be realistic about what you can do in a day. Make a list of things to do and determine the best time to take on each task. If you are a morning person, address the most challenging projects in the morning, leaving rote tasks for later in the day.

Depending on how you use it, technology can either help or hinder your effort to manage your work. Laptop computers, email, fax machines, and Blackberries make it easier than ever to work evenings and on weekends. Use these tools to increase the flexibility of your schedule, not to increase the amount of time you work.

Work flow management is essential to efficient use of time. Stick to your schedule; set realistic deadlines for yourself and honor them. Allow yourself ample blocks of uninterrupted time. If you have an office door, close it when you want to get something done. Don't let co-workers interrupt you for unimportant reasons. Rather than responding to telephone calls and email messages as they come in, set aside time every day to respond to all the messages in one session.

If you don't seriously manage your workload, you will find that your workload will manage you – and you won't like it. Nobody is supposed to work every day, even if God is in your workplace. Honoring the Sabbath brings people closer to God, as well as preserving a sustainable pace of work for them.

Congregational worship is a traditional component of the Sabbath. Career-driven people often find themselves thinking about work while they attend worship services. Knowing they should be focusing on God, such thought typically brings a certain amount of guilt to these mental wanderers. Congregants should be listening to the preacher, the thinking goes. Prayers and hymns should be offered with heavenly thoughts, not ideas for balancing the budget. The GEO Principle, however, can alleviate a measure of that guilt.

If you bring God to work, it becomes clear that it is acceptable to bring work to God. Congregational worship is a suitable time to offer up to God your work-related worries. Are you dealing with a spreadsheet problem in accounting? Offer it up to God. Describe it and outline the options for resolution. Concerned about market pressures, hiring conditions or real estate prices? Share your fears with the Almighty. Pray for discernment. God wants to help you, and that starts with you asking for his help. The GEO Principle acknowledges that God wants to assist you with professional concerns as much as he wants to help with any other concerns.

Although Sabbath might invoke thoughts of a weekly schedule, it can be considered in the context of longer periods of rest. In Mark 6:31-32, Jesus invites the apostles into retreat. A good vacation helps a person clear the head, experience new things and grow closer to family members or companions. Periodic rejuvenation is essential for maintaining physical, emotional, intellectual and spiritual health.

Unfortunately, as Western culture seems to develop ever more materialistic, Americans are actually taking less vacation time now than ever. Almost half of 730 executives in the United States who responded to a 2003 survey by Management Recruiters International said they did not expect to use their vacation time that year. Also in 2003, Expedia.com estimated Americans piled up $21 billion in unused vacation time. In 2004, a Harris Interactive survey showed 30 percent of employed Americans gave up vacation days.[12]

"The idea of somebody going away for two weeks is really becoming a thing of the past," a spokesperson for the American Automobile Association told the *New York Times*. "It's kind of sad, really, that people can't seem to leave their jobs anymore."[13]

Laws in the United States do not require companies to give employees paid time off. Vacation policies in U.S. companies typically equate to ten or fifteen days off per year, depending on how long the person has worked at the company. American workers fortunate enough to get the ten federal holidays off, end up with twenty to twenty-five days off per year, compared with our French counterparts, who typically get forty days off, or Japanese workers, who get thirty-five days off.

Planning for vacations is as important as planning workflow. Even though you may be entitled to a vacation, you have to take deliberate steps to assure you get the time off. If you always find yourself too busy to take vacation time, consider whether you may be a workaholic, susceptible to accompanying physical ailments such as sleep disorders and high blood pressure. A number of online self-tests are readily accessible to help people anonymously assess their situation.

Even if you are healthy, unceasing work easily devolves into drudgery. Don't allow yourself to work like the animals. Be the human that God wants you to be by regularly honoring the Sabbath with rest. While the commercial world is an important theater in the drama of life, it is not the only show in town. Obligations to work colleagues and customers should be considered in the context of obligations to spouse, children, relatives and neighbors. Weekends away from the workplace provide valuable rest; annual or semi-annual rests of a week or more have further rejuvenating effect.

Consider ❭ ❭ ❭

1. The average person has 112 hours of waking time a week, assuming eight hours of nightly sleep. Including preparatory time at home and your commute, how many hours a week are you devoting to work? Do the total work hours equal more than half your waking hours? Do you think you are working too much, or too little?

2. How much vacation time have you taken each of the last two years? Did you let earned vacation time go unused?

3. If it is difficult for you to get away for vacation, what could you do to make it easier?

ACTION STEPS ❭ ❭ ❭

1. Take a serious look at your daily routine and consider whether any duties or activities can be eliminated to make time for something more important.

2. Plan a vacation of at least three days for sometime in the next three months. It doesn't have to involve costly travel, and you could plan it over a weekend so it requires you to miss only one day of work.

3. Plan a vacation of at least seven days for sometime in the next year.

For Further Consideration, Read ❱ ❱ ❱

Chained to the Desk: a Guidebook for Workaholics, Their Partners, and Children, and the Clinicians Who Treat Them by Bryan Robinson (NYU Press, 2007)

CHAPTER EIGHTEEN

Take a Sabbatical

ONE OF THE ways Moses instructed the Israelites to honor the Sabbath was to acknowledge a "Sabbath year" every seventh year. Farmers were to allow their land to go fallow every seventh year in order for it to rejuvenate. Working people, like farmland, need periodic rejuvenation beyond one or two weeks. Ideally, everyone in the commercial world would take a lengthy break every seven years.

Sabbaticals, which go far beyond the regularly scheduled break from work, can foster intense personal development. The academic world, where professors can receive up to a year off with pay, has this figured out. A limited number of people in other professions get the opportunity to take a few months off from their regular routine; they work for firms that have formal sabbatical programs. Watson Wyatt, a benefits consulting company, estimates that about twenty percent of large companies offer some form of a sabbatical program.[14]

Regardless of whether one is fortunate enough to work for a company that offers sabbaticals, everyone – no matter what their work or family situation – should consider taking a meaningful sabbatical during their working life. While a seven-year timeframe is typically associated with the concept of Sabbath, the Israelites also acknowledged a Jubilee year, which took place once every fifty years (Leviticus 25:8-10). It was an extra special commemoration freeing people from servitude every "seven times seven years." This Jubilee model is more practically applicable to people in the work world today; just as the Israelites took the Jubilee seriously, American workers should take a sabbatical no less frequently than once every fifty years. (And don't wait the entire fifty years to take it!)

A break of six weeks to twelve months is not primarily about rest, the way a week off is. A sabbatical experience is about trying something different, learning something new, or venturing into something experimental. This is the opportunity to write a manuscript, build a log cabin, learn a foreign language, ride a bicycle across the state, read all the works of Shakespeare, volunteer at a museum, travel or train for a marathon. The point is, a sabbatical provides the time to do something meaningful outside your routine.

Arranging your life in order to create such an opportunity is difficult but doable. Because we live in a culture that focuses largely on the short term, most people don't look several years forward. Companies focused on the current quarter's earnings don't generally think about their employees taking time off, other than for a short vacation. It is unlikely that your boss is going to hand you a sabbatical. You have to make it happen.

Start by figuring out what you want to do. Determine the length of time off you want and figure out when would be the best time to take it. Determine for yourself the means by which you expect to live. Will you use savings or does your company offer salary continuation for certain kinds of leave? Some companies, for example, may continue to pay you during your sabbatical if the time off is deemed family leave. Then think about what your absence will mean for your employer. How will your work get done? Will a colleague pick up your work, can a temporary employee be brought in, or can the work remain stalled while you are away? Consider all these questions before approaching your boss, at least one year before the onset of the sabbatical.

Some employers will work with you while others will not. Even if you work for a sympathetic employer, however, you need to be flexible. The employer might suggest a different time frame; it might guarantee a job when you return, but not necessarily the same job. Or, the employer might say: "Absolutely not. Forget it!" In this case, an employee has to look hard at his or her career and decide what's important in life.

Anyone can take a sabbatical if they are willing to quit their job and go unemployed for the duration of the time off. This is a difficult option, but it is feasible for people who have financial support from a spouse, relative or personal savings. A subsequent return to the workforce upon completion of a sabbatical may mean a different job, perhaps even at a lower salary. This is a significant cost but the benefits of a rejuvenating sabbatical also are significant.

Consider ❱ ❱ ❱

1. Do you know anyone outside of the academic world who has taken a sabbatical? How did they do it? Talk to them about the experience. Ask how difficult it was to plan, what they did with the time off, and how the experience affected them once they returned to work.

2. If you could take a sabbatical, what would you want to do and how much time would it take? How might your company get by without you during that time?

3. Is it realistic for you to consider quitting your job and getting another one after completing a sabbatical? Why or why not?

ACTION STEPS ❱ ❱ ❱

1. Make plans to take a sabbatical within the next five years.

2. After you take the sabbatical, tell others about the experience. Help your colleagues do something similar for themselves.

For Further Consideration, Read ❱ ❱ ❱

Power Sabbatical: The Break That Makes a Difference by Robert Scott Levine (Findhorn Press, 2007)

CHAPTER NINETEEN

Debt and the Sabbath

MOSES INSTRUCTED THAT all debts be released during the Sabbath year (Deuteronomy 15:1-2). Such an edict kept people from entering into a lifestyle of debt. Ongoing financial indebtedness was considered a form of financial servitude to be avoided. Financial enslavement, since the time of Moses, has impeded people from entering into the Sabbath rest.

Even a cursory study of the Sabbath prompts an examination of debt, financial or otherwise, in each of our lives. If you owe somebody something, consider how you might pay off that debt as soon as possible. If somebody owes you something, consider how you might help them clear the debt up; don't let the indebtedness go on forever.

In modern American culture, debt is a valuable tool. Credit cards, home equity lines of credit, mortgages and other loans help people smooth over personal cash flow anomalies, purchase homes and pay for college. Most people today would find it very difficult to establish their households without tapping into some form of credit.

Debt, however, like work, can be seductive. Many people borrow too much and get themselves in situations where they cannot repay. Regardless of the spirit of Deuteronomy 15, no modern-day creditor is willingly going to let a borrower off the hook. Prudent use of credit means never borrowing money without a plan for repaying it. Financial experts typically advise people to limit credit card use to major purchases; credit card bills should be paid off during the grace period whenever possible. Couples who finance a home with one income rather than two build a cushion into their personal financial situation. Car buyers willing to settle for a model that can be purchased with savings avoid trouble that could befall the buyer who finances over four or five years.

If your life is unaffected by unmanageable levels of debt, praise God – by helping those who may be wrestling with burdensome debt. Living in a relationship with God is not just about being happy for your personal situation, but about helping others.

Consider that while no one has the right to poke into someone else's personal financial affairs, from time to time one becomes aware of another's financial difficulties. Parents, for example, know the level of debt their college children may have. A relative might mention at a family gathering that he is struggling with mounting credit card bills. At work, you might hear a colleague complain about an unexpected increase in the rent at home. People of means should not let these clues go unnoticed.

If you are in a position to lend someone, say, a thousand dollars, consider doing so. If that person has to use a credit card to borrow a thousand dollars they are going to pay somewhere around two hundred dollars in interest over the course of a year. If you lend them the money at, say, four percent, you could save your borrower one hundred and sixty dollars.

Lending anyone money is a dicey endeavor. People with comfortable balances in their savings accounts don't typically achieve such security by making risky moves with their money. But helping someone through a financial hardship is a real and tangible way to bring meaning to Sabbath.

If you ever find yourself considering lending money to someone:

❭ Put the agreement in writing, spelling out terms such as interest rate, monthly payment, and when you expect the loan to be paid off. (Take a clue from Deuteronomy and don't lend money for more than seven years.)

❭ Charge some rate of interest. (Depending on the situation, consider a rate slightly higher than the rate you could get on a savings account. The point of charging interest is not for the lender to make money, but for the borrower to understand this is a serious loan.)

❭ Consider what will happen if the debt cannot be repaid. How will it affect you and those who depend on you? (If it would affect your household in a material way, you shouldn't make the loan.) How will it affect your relationship with the borrower? Would you be able to maintain a friendly relationship with him or her?

❭ If the borrower cannot repay the loan, can you offer the borrower work to pay down the debt? For example, could the borrower mow your lawn for a year to repay a five hundred dollar debt?

The internet has made it possible for people to connect with at least two other kinds of borrowers: over-extended Americans and poor people living in Third World countries. Prosper.com and Zopa.com are social networking sites of sorts designed to match Americans who need money with people who have money. Sites such as Microplace.com, Kiva.org and GrameenFoundation.org facilitate micro-lending to grassroots entrepreneurs across the globe.

If you are in a position to fund loans through a website such as Prosper, you are in position to help someone reduce their debt load. Typically, the people who post loan requests on Prosper have large outstanding credit card balances, paying interest rates of twenty percent or more. Their goal is to refinance at a more manageable interest rate. People willing to lend even as little as fifty dollars can help borrowers substantially lower the cost of their debt.

The beneficiaries of micro-loans have a much more difficult challenge than Americans who have over-spent on credit. Micro-loans typically are aimed at the poorest of the poor – people who make less than one dollar per day. Lifting people out of poverty is a difficult proposition, but in some cases a micro-loan is the key. Hope for the City, a Minneapolis-based charity, runs a micro-loan program in India. Their loans range from one hundred dollars to five hundred dollars. One Indian used a Hope for the City loan to buy an iron and started a laundry business. Another used the money to buy a water buffalo; the milk feeds a family and provides a small but steady income.

The human family is enormous; God invites all of us into the Sabbath rest in order to develop our relationship with him. Every human wrestles with something that holds them back. For some, financial stress diminishes the prospects for periodic rest. The GEO Principle means working in a way that honors the Sabbath. Manage your debt so you don't enslave yourself. If your own financial affairs are sufficiently ordered, consider what you might do to help someone less fortunate. One of the best ways to work on your own journey into the Sabbath is to help others to get there as well.

Consider ❱ ❱ ❱

1. What is your attitude about debt? Is your own debt manageable? If not, what do you need to do to strengthen your financial footing?

2. Do you know someone struggling with debt? Could you do anything to help?

ACTION STEPS ❱ ❱ ❱

1. Track your income and expenses over several months and create a budget for your household.

2. Google the terms "peer to peer lending" and "micro-lending." Learn about options to help those struggling to keep out of debt or those who need capital. If you have the means, help where you can.

For Further Consideration, Read ❱ ❱ ❱

Banker to the Poor: Micro-lending and the Battle Against World Poverty by Muhammad Yuna (Public Affairs, 2003)

CHAPTER TWENTY

The Twilight Years

JUST AS THE American concept of retirement changed in the twentieth century, it is changing again in the early twenty-first century. The idea that one should cease work at age sixty-five in favor of full-time leisure funded by savings and Social Security is beginning to give way to fresh thinking about the role work plays in the last third of one's life. As life expectancy lengthens, people are increasingly seeking to maintain meaningful social engagement through full or part-time work arrangements well into their seventies and even eighties.

In his best-selling book "The Number," Lee Eisenberg cites AARP research that notes 70 percent of people still in the workforce plan to work at least part-time during the years traditionally considered for retirement. Some said they never plan to retire. More than two-thirds said the reason they want to continue to work is because that's how a person stays active, remains useful and has fun.[15]

In six hundred telephone interviews with small business owners across the country, Wells Fargo found 87 percent of them said they do not plan on a traditional retirement. Forty percent say they plan no reduction in work at all and will only stop working when they are forced to do so for health reasons.[16]

While a growing percentage of people may be returning to the idea of meaningful life-long commercial engagement, some people never rejected the idea in the first place. Many famous people have worked well into old age. Karol Wojtyla, better known as Pope John Paul II, was still traveling around the globe in his eighties; Ronald Reagan was president in his seventies; Alan Greenspan was chairman of the Federal Reserve Board until he was seventy-nine; Jessica Tandy and Hume Cronin, the celebrated husband and wife acting team, performed well into old age; and Jack Dreyfus, best known for his mutual funds, was still coming into his midtown Manhattan office in his nineties. John Gagliardi, one of the most successful college football coaches ever, coached his sixtieth season in 2008 when he was eighty-two years old.

Bill George, former CEO of a Fortune 500 medical devices company, wrote a book called "True North" in which he identifies several business leaders, including fourteen over the age of seventy, and nineteen in their sixties. George's oldest interviewee was Zyg Nagorski, who runs the Center for International Leadership; he was ninety-three years old.[17]

You don't have to be famous or powerful to work well into old age. The Associated Press published a story in August 2007 about several people in their nineties who still held jobs.[18] Pete Perillo, ninety-two, is a judicial marshal for the Superior Court in Stamford, Connecticut; Grace Wiles, ninety-seven, works twenty-five hours a week in a shoe repair shop in Maryland; and Sally Gordon, ninety-eight, works as the assistant sergeant at arms for the Nebraska state legislature. The article says that 104-year-old Waldo McBurney, a bookkeeper in Kansas, is the nation's oldest worker.

According to the U.S. Labor Department, about 6.4 percent of Americans seventy-five or older – slightly more than one million people – were working in 2006. About 3.4 percent of Americans eighty or older – or 318,000 people – were in the work force that year.

The number of older people in the workplace will grow, simply as a matter of necessity, observes the *Wall Street Journal.* In many countries, there aren't enough people under the age of sixty-five to sustain the existing commercial structure. In Japan, more than 20 percent of the population is already older than sixty-five. The same thing is true in Italy. Twenty percent of Germany's population will be older than sixty-five in 2009. Although immigration keeps the workforce younger by comparison in the United States, even here 20 percent of the population will be sixty-five or older by 2036.[19]

Researching his book, Bill George interviewed Lord John Browne, the CEO of British Petroleum. George quotes Browne: "I don't believe in retirement. The idea seems a touch out of date." Browne said that when he steps down as CEO at the age of sixty, he will seek a new business challenge.

In "The Gifted Boss," columnist Dale Dauten writes about a re-tired executive, Vince Ciccarelli, who went back to work because he was bored. A mail-order gift business in Minneapolis initially gave Ciccarelli a temporary assignment. He did so well the owners didn't want him to leave. "You can't leave…we need you," Dauten quotes Susan, one of the company's owners. "Ciccarelli's reaction was to throw back his head and laugh. Susan described that moment, that laugh, by saying 'I knew then that I could give him what he needed – to be needed.'" Dauten went on to describe the unique employ-ment arrangement they struck, which included a three o'clock in the afternoon quitting time four days a week, and only a half-day commitment on Fridays.[20]

Retirement at a pre-determined age is a twentieth century idea for people who see little meaning in their work beyond a paycheck. People seeking meaningful social engagement in the commercial arena regardless of their age are living a key component of the GEO Principle. Those who see their work as a very important way to grow closer to God set the pace of their work according to their physical ability, not their age. Granted, in many cases, age and work pace are related. That pace would naturally slow as a person nears the end of life but for many people, age sixty-five is two decades or more away from the physical deterioration that would necessitate the cessation of work.

Many people pledge that upon retirement they will devote themselves to volunteer work; this laudable ambition results in a continuation of very valuable work. Meaningful work is more about engaging in purposeful endeavor than it is about levels of compensation. Staying engaged in work does not necessarily mean staying at the same job or company forever. Management guru Stephen Covey advises "retire from your job but never from meaningful projects. If you want to live a long life, you need *eustress*, that is, a deep sense of meaning and of contribution to worthy projects and causes, particularly your intergenerational family. If you want to die early, retire to golf and fishing and sit around swallowing prescriptions and occasionally seeing your grandkids."[21]

People are increasingly finding the best way to ensure engagement in meaningful projects is through work in the commercial arena. Without a commitment to an employer – and the accompanying co-workers, customers and industry colleagues – many people find it difficult to muster the discipline necessary to sustain a meaningful engagement.

To be sure, the paycheck plays an important role in all this. With standard retirement planning shifting toward defined contribution formats over the old defined benefit formats, people are finding it more difficult to secure decades of time off for leisure. In that Wells Fargo survey, 43 percent of business owners said they fear they will not have enough money to retire. Ever since someone dreamed up the idea of leisure-filled retirement, people have worried over their ability to attain such a thing. Mutual fund companies and other sectors of the personal investment industry have capitalized on that anxiety.

Christians know the story about the man who had so much grain that he built bigger silos to store it for years to come (Luke 12:16-21). He died the very next day and never enjoyed any of the wealth he had saved up. The point of this story is to remind us not to take the gift of life for granted and not to store up wealth for our own selfish reasons.

Before jumping to conclusions, however, consider the story of the bridesmaids who were waiting through the night for the groom (Matthew 25:1-13). Some of them brought extra oil for their lamps and others didn't. The women who planned ahead – saved for the future – were rewarded, while those who did not plan ahead were punished. Given the seeming conflict between these two stories, what are we supposed to do: Are we, or aren't we, supposed to plan ahead and save for the future?

The answer, of course, is somewhere in between these two extremes. The man with all the grain was planning to store enough wealth to last him years, perhaps decades. The bridesmaids were planning only for what they needed. They wanted to make sure they had enough to get through the night. While the bridesmaids seemed to be exercising prudence, the man building the grain bins seemed to be flirting with greed. He seemed to be setting himself up for self-centered living.

The two stories pose a worthwhile framework for people to consider their own retirement planning goals. We can ask: "Am I being greedy or prudent with my savings?"

A prudent level of savings designed to cover emergencies and fund end-of-life needs, perhaps supplemented with long-term care insurance, makes eminent sense for anyone. People short-change themselves and their families, however, by focusing too much on retirement savings when they are in their forties, thirties or even twenties. We all know people who decide to limit their family size because they believe they can't afford to raise more than one or two kids and save for their own retirement at the same time. Others say they can't afford to care for their elderly parents while they continue to sock away thousands of dollars per year in a retirement plan. What our culture has come to consider traditional retirement is a costly proposition, not only in terms of the money required to live in old age, but also in terms of the opportunities and responsibilities that get neglected while that money is being accumulated.

During the latter half of the twentieth century, the promise of ongoing leisure was enough to make most people forget about the prospect of working past age sixty-five. Increasingly, though, people are changing their expectations about the twilight years. They are thinking more seriously about what they want, and for many of them that includes work. The social interaction of the work environment gives many people the opportunity to grow deeper in their faith. The fortunate ones figure that out mid-career or sooner.

Consider ❱ ❱ ❱

1. What does retirement mean to you?

2. Do you expect to stop working someday? When? Why?

3. What do you expect to do after you stop working?

4. To what extent will you remain engaged in the world during the latter years of your life?

5. If there is something you want to do during the latter years of your life, what is preventing you from doing it now?

6. How would your relationship with God be affected by a transition from a lifestyle centered around work to a lifestyle centered around leisure?

7. How much money are you saving for retirement? How is your effort to fund retirement impacting you and your family today?

ACTION STEPS ❱ ❱ ❱

1. Identify as many people as you can age 70 or older who still work 35 hours or more per week. Talk to them. Ask them why they haven't retired.

2. Talk to your spouse about expectations for your relationship and your household once you reach the years typically associated with retirement.

For Further Consideration, Read ❱ ❱ ❱

Successful Aging by John W. Rowe and Robert L. Kahn (Dell Publishing, 1998)

CHAPTER TWENTY-ONE

Retirement and Social Security

MEANINGFUL WORKPLACE ENGAGEMENT through the "retirement" years is not only becoming more common, but it is becoming more commonly recognized as worthwhile. In addition to cultivating a sense of purpose and well-being, late-in-life work offers significant social benefits that go far beyond the individual and those surrounding him. Companies benefit from the experience of older workers; those workers become an inspiration to younger industry participants; and customers enjoy greater continuity in service.

And, the benefits are even more widespread than that. Consider the potential impact on the nation's system of Social Security.

Life-long work reduces a person's dependence on Social Security. This is freeing for the individual and helpful for the future of our country, which really means our children and grandchildren. People who work long past the standard retirement age can continue to earn an income so they don't need to rely on Social Security income. Rethinking the role of Social Security in your life is the kind of concept that becomes possible for people living the GEO Principle.

In today's culture, it may sound absolutely absurd to talk about foregoing Social Security benefits, but if you don't need them, why take them? Prudent investors have a saying: "Bulls and bears do okay, pigs get slaughtered." In other words, invest with the idea of making what you need, but don't get greedy. If you don't need something, then leave it for those who do.

As surprising as it may seem, there already are people who hand over their rightful Social Security checks. The *New York Times* profiled a growing group of people who regularly donate their Social Security checks to charity. These Social Security recipients don't need the money themselves and choose to give the money to people who really need it.[22]

Another option is simply to decline the money. If you don't take your Social Security benefits, you will be slowing the growth of the U.S. federal deficit. Although the Social Security Trust Fund is, technically, separate from the federal budget, they are linked because the federal government borrows money from the fund to cover its own expenses. That means your money is not in the Social Security Trust Fund to return to you upon your retirement. Future benefits will be funded by payments from future workers. Given the shifting demographics of our country, where the number of people entering retirement age is growing faster than the number of people entering the workforce, the current Social Security system is unsustainable. As it is currently set up, Social Security will exhaust its reserves by 2042.[23]

Strangely, we have developed a system in this country where healthy, able-bodied people have come to expect a monthly stipend in their senior years – regardless of whether they need the money. In the middle part of the twentieth century, when the birth rate guaranteed more people entering the workforce than leaving it, elected officials could responsibly set up a system where workers partially fund retirees. But such an arrangement makes no sense with today's demographics. Former Federal Reserve Board Chairman Alan Greenspan has commented on this: "By almost any measure, the additional savings required to take care of the surge in retirees is sufficiently large to raise serious questions about whether the federal government will be able to meet the retirement commitments already made."[24]

If you paid into the Social Security system your entire life, of course you have a right to the benefits. Sustaining the current benefits structure, however, will require adjustment: Wages collected to fund benefits will have to increase, payment of benefits will have to be delayed, and/or benefits will have to be reduced. The political debate over the options won't be pretty, but people who don't need the benefits can alleviate some of the pressure by voluntarily foregoing payments while their own wages sustain them into old age. If a typical Social Security retirement benefits recipient collects twelve thousand dollars per year, they could save the country nearly a quarter of a million dollars over a couple of decades – only a drop in a sea of federal debt, but significant, nonetheless, from a single American citizen.

While Social Security is an incendiary political topic, the GEO Principle is not about politics. The GEO Principle is about living a relationship with God. Such a life is fruitful beyond all conventional thinking. People who successfully integrate their faith with their work lives will make an enormous impact on our world; possibilities emerge when we bring God to work which simply are unimaginable when we leave him home.

Consider ❱ ❱ ❱

1. Consider the pros and cons of the Social Security system in this country. How important is it to maintain the system in its current form? Are there attractive alternatives?

2. Does the thought of foregoing Social Security benefits make you angry? Why?

3. Have you ever voluntarily given up something valuable that was rightfully yours for the sake of the greater common good?

ACTION STEP ❱ ❱ ❱

Develop a plan for the last third of your life that includes paid work and does not include Social Security income.

For Further Consideration, Read ❱ ❱ ❱

The Age of Turbulence: Adventures in a New World by Alan Greenspan (The Penguin Press, 2007) Start with Chapter 18.

Integration versus Balance

TAKE TIME TO consider what the world would be like if everyone brought God to work. Faith-filled people will legitimately disagree about the details of all the possible scenarios; God has a unique plan for each person so the GEO Principle will mean different things to different people. Speculation about a world in which God is in Every Occupation, nonetheless, spawned this book, and I want to conclude by sharing the experience of my effort to put the GEO Principle into practice.

Some people are called to high-profile social causes or charitable work that saves thousands of people from disease or injustice. I admire people who bring health care to the poor or teach in inner-city schools. I used to consider my own, far less altruistic career path to be somewhat inferior to these selfless vocational commitments. The GEO Principle, however, has helped me see the God-glorifying opportunity in all honest work. The meaning I used to think could only be found in non-profit work emerges in my own commercial career as I try to bring God to my job. Journeying toward God is less about doing meaningful work and more about making work meaningful.

I run a modest publishing company; it is as important for me to live the GEO Principle in a small office environment as it is for a doctor to live the GEO Principle in a county hospital or a teacher to live it in an urban school building, or for a Fortune 500 CEO to live it in the global marketplace.

At my company, I am trying to create an environment where my colleagues can live the GEO Principle too. I'm trying to live by the suggestions listed in this book. For example, one way I am trying to love my employees is by respecting their schedules. I do this by ignoring the clock. Employees are allowed to adjust their schedules and calendars as they like, as long as the work gets done on time. They are free to tend to non-work obligations during the day if they need to. If employees find it makes sense for them to handle personal affairs at work, they get no complaint from me. Office equipment is there for them to use as they see fit, even home projects. Trust – one of the greatest byproducts of the GEO Principle – makes this possible.

I can't help but pray for the people I love, so I pray for all my employees in addition to my customers, vendors and other business contacts. Recall that prayer is one of the three practical ways to bring the GEO Principle to work. Being an example is the second practical way to bring God to work, although I must confess that I am inspired by the example of those around me far more than my own example inspires them. When I see the extent to which my colleagues help each other or go out of their way for others, I am humbled. These examples open the door to the third practical way to bring God to work – conversation. Acknowledgement and affirmation open the way to meaningful conversations which stir thought and sometimes even provoke action.

As I grew more comfortable with the prayer-example-conversation methodology, the GEO Principle lifespan model began to make more sense. As I incorporated eternity into my thinking, immediacy became more important. When I started to think about how important the afterlife is, I began to realize how important life on earth is. And it's short. Despite all the actuarial tables, there are no guarantees about life expectancy. And even if a person could be assured of living to be one hundred years old, that's not a lot of time against the backdrop of eternity.

My desire to retire has diminished as I have contemplated the GEO Principle. I am not willing to endure decades of drudgery for the promise of a leisure-filled future. Dividing my life into distinct time periods – one dedicated to work and another devoted to recreation – is not the answer. Why should people wait until the last third of their life to find the happiness they want all along? The cultural assumption is that happiness comes from the absence of work, but happiness is really the byproduct of love. I am interacting with people I love at work. I'd be silly to think they all love me but certainly if God is commanding me to love my neighbor, that includes my office colleagues, the guy who fixes the copier, my competitors, vendors, customers, and creditors. It is through these important, demanding and loving relationships that I am developing a relationship with God – and finding happiness today. I don't need to wait until retirement.

The GEO Principle, furthermore, helped me to see the Sisyphus-like nature of retirement planning. It's a treadmill and I have hopped off. Of course, I am putting away a little money in case I can't work in my latter days, but I am not aiming for a big number so I can retire in my fifties or sixties. The multi-billion dollar retirement planning industry encourages us to chase a number, that is, a bank balance large enough to fund thirty or more years of idleness. Retirement planning is important if you expect your actions during the last third of your life to be significantly different from the actions of the middle third of your life – a discordant prospect for folks who find a meaningful way to live the middle third of their lives.

One of the fruits of the GEO Principle for me has been emancipation from that retirement savings account. I don't need to save money for the living expenses I may incur during my seventies if I plan to work during those years. It would be scandalous for someone intent on retiring to dismiss his need to save for it, but absent such plans, there is no need. If I maintain my middle-age lifestyle – work and all – into old age, I can use more of my earnings now.

Bringing God to work has enabled me to balance my life. We all hear about people seeking balance – an elusive notion in a world of cluttered calendars and multi-tasking. Perhaps the greatest benefit of the GEO Principle for me has been an understanding of how to achieve sustainable balance.

Think of a balance scale with two pans teetering on a fulcrum. Imagine balancing objects on the two pans until the pointer indicates equality. Now apply this model to life. With a lot of effort, I might have been able to attain some semblance of balance – family, church and volunteer commitments piled up on one side, and work commitments piled up on the other. But then something would always happen. Work got busier and family life changed with a new school year or more taxing demands from the kids. The scale would fall way out of balance.

As long as my faith life and work life competed for my attention, I felt pulled apart and out of balance. As long as I kept the light of faith under a bushel basket at work, I found my work to be forever encroaching on my home life. I resented my work and I was unhappy with my home life. But once I started to integrate my home life with my work life, things changed. As I began to lift the bushel basket from the light of faith at work, my home life and work life began to balance. I no longer sensed two competing interests in my life. I no longer felt myself in a tug-of-war between home and work. The scales came into balance.

The balance scale analogy affirms my experience. Think of how much easier it is to achieve balance if you put the same thing – a mixture of faith and work – on both pans of the scale. When there was tension between work and faith, I pictured a pile of rocks representing work on one side of the scale and a pile of sand representing faith on the other side. Balance was very difficult to achieve with different things on each side of the scale. But combine the sand and rocks in each pan on both sides of the scale, and balance becomes much easier to achieve. With integration of faith and work, the scale balances.

God is the ultimate work colleague. He can do wonders, even in corporate America. But he is counting on you. Bring God along every day you go to work.

End Notes

[1] Patrick Lencioni, *The Three Signs of a Miserable Job: A Fable for Managers (and Their Employees)* (Jossey-Bass, San Francisco, 2007) page 253.

[2] All quotes from David Gergen in this book originate from an interview conducted Sept. 17, 2007, in Des Moines, Iowa.

[3] Brent Kallsestad, "2 in 5 Bosses Don't Keep Their Word, Florida State University Survey Shows" *Associated Press*, Jan. 1, 2007.

[4] James L. Johnson, senior pastor at Good Shepherd Church, Camarillo, Calif. Survey conducted spring 2007.

[5] Alex Johnson, "Faith-at-work Movement Finds a Home: Building a Silicon Valley of the Soul in Northwest Arkansas" MSNBC.com March 21, 2005.

[6] Jim Collins, *Good to Great: Why Some Companies Make the Leap...and Others Don't*, (HarperCollins Publishing, Inc., New York, 2001) page 39.

[7] www.nifplay.org

[8] William Carden speaking at the Day with the Superintendent, hosted by the Iowa Division of Banking in West Des Moines, April 28, 2005.

[9] Thomas Friedman, *The World Is Flat: A brief history of the twenty-first century, updated and expanded*, (Farrar, Straus and Giroux, New York, 2005) pages 375-376.

[10] ibid, page 302

[11] Pope Benedict XVI speaking at a Sunday address from Castelgandolfo on August 20, 2006 – referring to the writing of St. Bernard of Chiaravalle.

[12] www.braunconsulting.com/bcg/newsletters/winter2004/winter20044. html

[13] Timothy Egan, "The Rise of Shrinking-Vacation Syndrome," *New York Times,* August 20, 2006.

[14] Jane Bennett Clark, "A Pause That Refreshes," *Kiplinger's Personal Finance*, March 2006.

[15] Lee Eisenberg, *The Number: A Completely Different Way to Think About the Rest of Your Life*. (Free Press, New York, 2006) page 69-70.

[16] *Small Business Owners' Concern: Not Enough Money for Retirement* Press release issued by Wells Fargo & Company, San Francisco, January 29, 2008.

[17] Bill George, *True North, Discover your Authentic Leadership* (Jossey-Bass, San Francisco, 2007) pages 24-25.

[18] John Christoffersen, "Working Past 90: Many Americans in Their Golden Years Have Forsaken the Gold Watch and Stayed on the Job – Some Because They Want to Work, Others Because They Must" *Associated Press*, published in the *Saint Paul Pioneer Press* August 15, 2007.

[19] Sebastian Moffett, "Fast-Aging Japan Keeps Its Elders On the Job Longer," *Wall Street Journal*, page 1, June 17, 2005.

[20] Dale Dauten, *The Gifted Boss*, (William Morrow and Company, Inc., New York, 1999) pages 79-80.

[21] Stephen R. Covey, *The Eighth Habit*, (Free Press, New York, 2004) page 63.

[22] John Leland, "Doing Good By Doing Without Social Security," *New York Times*, April 3, 2005.

[23] "Social Security Facts at a Glance," Economic Policy Institute, www.epinet.org

[24] Alan Greenspan, *The Age of Turbulence: Adventures in a New World* (The Penguin Press, New York, 2007) page 413.

Scripture texts in *The GEO Principle* are from either:

• *The Holy Bible, New King James Version*, (Thomas Nelson, Inc., Nashville, Tenn.) 1982, or

• *The New American Bible*, by the Confraternity of Christian Doctrine, (Catholic Book Publishing Co., New York) 1970.

ABOUT THE AUTHOR

TOM BENGTSON is a writer, speaker and entrepreneur living in Minneapolis with his wife Susan and their four children. Tom is president of NFR Communications, a publishing company specializing in trade and custom publications. Tom, an award-winning journalist, has covered business for more than twenty years.

In 2008, the newspaper for the archdiocese of Saint Paul and Minneapolis honored Tom with a "Leading with Faith" award.

Tom's first book was a memoir called *Emerging Son* in which he addresses themes common to young men growing into middle age. A 1983 graduate of the University of Minnesota, Tom studied English and French to obtain a liberal arts degree. Tom's other interests include sailing and aviation.

Tom can be contacted via email through The GEO Principle web site, www.GEOprinciple.com, which contains numerous resources for readers trying to implement the concepts presented in this book.